To my wife, Claudia; my parents, Warren and Eva Westcott; and my wife's parents, Tony and Marcelle Gance; for their prayers, support, and encouragement

STRENGTH FITNESS

STRENGTH FITNESS

Physiological Principles and Training Techniques

Wayne Westcott

South Shore YMCA

WCB Brown & Benchmark
PUBLISHERS

Madison, Wisconsin • Dubuque, Iowa

Book Team

Executive Editor *Ed Bartell*
Editor *Scott Spoolman*
Developmental Editor *Kassi Radomski*
Production Editor *Patricia A. Schissel*
Visuals/Design Developmental Consultant *Marilyn A. Phelps*
Visuals/Design Freelance Specialist *Mary L. Christianson*
Marketing Manager *Pamela S. Cooper*
Advertising Coordinator *Susan J. Butler*
Production Manager *Beth Kundert*

WCB Brown & Benchmark

A Division of Wm. C. Brown Communications, Inc.

Executive Vice President/General Manager *Thomas E. Doran*
Vice President/Editor in Chief *Edgar J. Laube*
Vice President/Marketing and Sales Systems *Eric Ziegler*
Director of Production *Vickie Putman Caughron*
Director of Custom and Electronic Publishing *Chris Rogers*

Wm. C. Brown Communications, Inc.

President and Chief Executive Officer *G. Franklin Lewis*
Vice President, Operations *James H. Higby*
Corporate Senior Vice President and Chief Financial Officer *Robert Chesterman*
Corporate Senior Vice President and President of Manufacturing *Roger Meyer*

Cover design by Sailer & Cook Creative Services

Cover photo courtesy of Wayne Westcott

Copyedited by Mary Agria

A Times Mirror Company

Library of Congress Catalog Card Number: 93–74747

ISBN 0–697–15270–7

Printed in the United States of America by Wm. C. Brown Communications, Inc.,
2460 Kerper Boulevard, Dubuque, IA 52001

10 9 8 7 6 5 4 3 2

Contents

Preface

Strength Fitness: Physiological Principals and Training Techniques is designed for exercise students and fitness professionals who desire practical information for developing safe, effective, and efficient strength-training programs.

The first chapters address strength-training benefits, strength potential, muscle physiology, and movement mechanics. The middle chapters deal with strength-training guidelines, strength-training effects, and equipment/safety concerns. Information follows on advanced training techniques, and programs for body-builders, strength builders, youth, and seniors. The text concludes with a chapter on strength-training considerations and an illustrated chapter on strength-training exercises for machine and free-weight equipment.

This edition is more comprehensive in scope, more concise in presentation, and more clear in description. It is a teaching text that bridges the gap between theory and practice, between physiological principles and training techniques. The information is meant for practical application, and should lead to safe and productive strength-training experiences.

The author acknowledges the ability and appreciates the assistance of those individuals most responsible for this book. They are: my editors, Kassi Radomski, Pat Schissel, and Mary Agria; my typist, Susan Ramsden; my artist, Leslie Willis; my photographer,

Sharon Townsend; my exercise models, Jerry Booker, Tracy D'Arpino, Mary Delmonico, Kyria DiPietro, Mike Kane, Robbie Kane, Susan Ramsden, Mike Savoie, Brian Wessner, Claudia Westcott, and Tiffany Zaniboni; and my YMCA executives, Mary Moore and Ralph Yohe. The author would also like to thank the following reviewers for their valuable feedback: Claudia Blackman, Southern Illinois University; Carol Christiansen, San Jose State University; and Jim Clemons, University of Southwestern Louisiana.

One

Introduction to Strength Training

Today, strength training is a popular physical activity that is often introduced in high school conditioning programs. Almost every community has modern strength-training facilities, and many home exercise rooms include some form of weight-training equipment. Nonetheless, general acceptance of strength training is a rather recent development, and few individuals really understand the benefits of regular strength exercise.

When asked about strength training, many people believe it is only important for bodybuilders, weight lifters, and athletes. They simply do not associate strength training or muscular fitness with average men and women.

Oddly enough, adults seem to fear having too much muscle. In fact, they should be concerned about having too little muscle. This is because men and women who do not perform regular strength exercise lose about five pounds of muscle every 10 years. The steady loss of muscle detracts from their personal appearance, decreases their physical capacity, and reduces their metabolic rate by 5 percent every decade.

This is a major reason Americans can eat the same amount of food but add fat weight year after year. With less muscle tissue, calories that were previously used for muscle maintenance are now deposited into fat storage.

Can strength training change this situation? Absolutely. Research participants routinely add about three pounds of muscle after two months of strength exercise. At the same time they lose up to 10 pounds of fat, depending on their attention to better dietary habits.

There are many other reasons everyone should perform sensible strength training. Strong low-back muscles are the best defense against low-back discomfort, a problem encountered by four out of every five Americans.

In addition, muscles function as the body's engine, chassis, and shock absorber. That is why well-conditioned muscles increase our physical capacity, enhance our personal appearance, and reduce our injury risk.

While a reasonable amount of effort and commitment are necessary to attain muscular fitness, strength training need not be a time-consuming activity. Generally speaking, 20 to 30 minutes two or three times per week of properly performed strength exercise is sufficient to develop all of our major muscle groups.

Brief History of Strength Training

In the early 1900s, weight-training rooms could be found in some YMCA facilities. This was consistent with the "muscular Christianity" theme of that era which advocated a strong spirit, mind, and body.

Unfortunately, weight-training rooms were typically dominated by a small group of strong males who seemed to intimidate those with less muscle-building potential. Weight-training rooms soon became the domain of competitive bodybuilders and weight lifters, and persons with other exercise objectives were seldom invited to participate.

Because naturally muscular individuals were found in weight rooms, strength training was thought to make people big and bulky. As a result of this incorrect assumption, average adults avoided strength exercise, and athletes were warned that weight training would make them slow, inflexible, and uncoordinated.

Following World War II, medical doctors experimented with strength exercise for injury rehabilitation and muscle rebuilding. These efforts were successful, and encouraged physical educators and coaches to include strength training in gym classes and sports conditioning programs.

At about the same time, new magazines devoted to body-building and weight lifting enhanced public awareness and acceptance of these activities. YMCAs expanded their strength training facilities, and free-weight gyms began to open throughout the country.

However, it was not until the 1970s, with the introduction of Nautilus machines and the accompanying training philosophy, that strength exercise became an attractive and accessible activity for average men and women. Since that time there has been a growing interest in strength training, particularly as it relates to a well-rounded fitness program.

Basic Philosophy of Strength Fitness

The basic philosophy of strength fitness focuses on training safety, training effectiveness, and training efficiency.

Safety: Regardless of how well a strength-training program may appear to work, it should be avoided if it has a high risk of injury. For example, fast weight lifting movements are not recommended because they place excessive stress on our muscles, tendons, and joint structures. Therefore, it is recommended that participants perform all strength exercises in a slow and controlled manner.

Effectiveness: Although different conditioning programs produce varying degrees of strength development, some are more effective than others. Consider traditional calisthenics such as push-ups and sit-ups. Because these body-weight exercises do not permit progressive increases in resistance, they produce only modest gains in strength. You can attain much better results by isolating specific muscle groups and progressively increasing the resistance with free-weights or machines.

Efficiency: If you are a busy person with limited time for physical conditioning, exercise efficiency is a very practical training consideration. For example, research shows that one set of exercise per muscle group produces excellent strength gains. Consequently, time-pressured individuals may be well-advised to follow a single-set strength-training program.

This text is titled *Strength Fitness* because its primary focus is sensible strength exercise for improving muscular fitness. It provides pertinent information for designing safe, effective, and efficient strength-training programs that enable all participants (male, female, young, old, athletic, unathletic) to look better, feel better, and function better. The following chapters present research results, training guidelines, and exercise protocols for successfully attaining higher levels of strength fitness.

Two

Strength-training Benefits

There are some activities you just feel good about performing because you know they are beneficial. Strength training is one of them. After completing a strength-training session, you experience a sense of physical accomplishment and personal well-being. That's because your muscles are your body engines, and a sound strength workout is similar to a good tune-up.

Primary Benefits

From a physical perspective, strength training produces a number of important adaptations in our musculoskeletal system. The primary response to progressive resistance exercise is an increase in the muscle proteins—specifically actin and myosin. The additional myoproteins form larger muscle fibers that have greater structural strength and greater contractile strength.

The stress applied to the muscles is transferred to the connective tissue (tendons and ligaments) and bones. This produces more collagen proteins in the tendons and ligaments, increasing their structural strength, and more osteoproteins in the bones, increasing their structural strength. The result is a well-developed musculoskeletal system that is both strong and injury-resistant.

Regular strength training also contributes more myofibrils per muscle fiber, more capillaries per muscle fiber, more intramuscular

5

energy stores, and better muscle fiber recruitment. These physiological adaptations are largely responsible for some important secondary benefits of strength exercise.

Secondary Benefits

Although strength training is essential for developing larger and stronger muscles, very few individuals have the potential to become competitive bodybuilders or weight lifters. Nonetheless, sensible strength training can benefit just about everyone with respect to improved physical capacity, higher metabolic function, greater athletic power, lower injury risk, enhanced personal appearance, and more self-satisfaction.

Physical Capacity

Physical capacity may be defined as our ability to perform work or exercise. While our heart functions as our fuel pump, our muscles serve as our engines. It is in our muscles where combustion takes place, energy is released, movement originates, and power is produced. Regular strength training increases our ability to perform work or exercise by building bigger and better muscular engines.

It is important to understand that every physical activity requires a certain percentage of our maximum physical capacity. Because our muscle strength and muscle endurance are closely related, more muscle strength automatically results in more muscle endurance. That is, strength training enables us to perform previously difficult tasks with considerably less effort. For example, if your maximum biceps strength is 25 pounds, carrying a 25-pound bag of groceries is an all-out effort. If you increase your biceps strength to 50 pounds, carrying the same bag of groceries requires only half of your available muscle force, making this task much easier to perform.

Even sedentary individuals use a significant amount of muscle strength during the course of a day. For example, one research study found that persons who simply sit at desks from 9:00 A.M. to 5:00 P.M. lose about 30 percent of their neck strength during that time (see figure 2.1). This is due to the fact that our neck muscles hold our 15-pound head erect throughout the day, and that can cause considerable muscle fatigue.

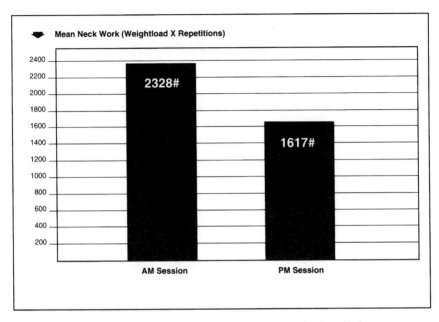

Figure 2.1 Neck strength for persons who sit at desks all day as tested at 9:00 A.M. and 5:00 P.M. (10 subjects)

Fortunately, it does not take long to experience the effects of progressive resistance exercise on physical capacity. Our research participants routinely increase their overall muscle performance by 45 to 65 percent after two months of strength training. Strong muscles enhance our physical capacity, and our physical capacity has a major influence on our daily lifestyle.

Metabolic Function

Because our muscles are our engines, strength training can have a significant influence on our metabolic function. Like other forms of exercise, strength training is a vigorous, calorie-burning activity. During a serious strength-training session, our heart rate, blood pressure, and energy metabolism increase considerably. Of course, this temporary elevation in energy consumption is experienced during other large muscle activities such as running, cycling, and swimming. However, shortly after we stop these activities, our metabolism returns to its resting level.

Strength training is different because it influences our resting metabolism as well as our exercise metabolism. This is due to the fact that strength training adds muscle tissue, and muscle tissue has a high energy requirement. The more muscle we develop, the more energy we need twenty-four hours a day for tissue maintenance and building processes. Even when we are asleep, our muscles are responsible for over 25 percent of our total calorie utilization.

After age 20, men and women who do not strength train lose approximately one-half pound of muscle every year of life through lack of use. This gradual reduction in muscle tissue is largely responsible for a 0.5 percent per year decrease in metabolism. Strength training is the best means for maintaining our muscle mass and metabolic function throughout middle age.

Strength exercise is unique due to its double effect on energy utilization. First, strength training produces a large increase in metabolic rate during the workout. Second, strength training adds more muscle tissue, which produces a small increase in metabolic rate throughout the day.

For these reasons, strength training is helpful in reducing body fat. In one study, 72 men and women followed the same diet guidelines and spent the same amount of time in an exercise program (30 minutes a day, three days a week). Twenty-two subjects spent all 30 minutes performing endurance exercise. The other 50 participants divided each workout into 15 minutes of endurance exercise and 15 minutes of strength exercise. After eight weeks, the subjects who did only endurance training lost four pounds of fat. The subjects who performed both endurance and strength exercise lost 10 pounds of fat and gained 2 pounds of muscle, for a 12-pound improvement in their body composition (see table 2.1). The better results obtained by the subjects who performed strength training were due in part to their increased muscle mass and metabolic rate.

A follow-up study with 90 men and women who performed 20 minutes of strength exercise and 20 minutes of endurance exercise three days a week produced similar results. After eight weeks, the subjects lost 9.5 pounds of fat and gained 3.5 pounds of muscle, for a 13-pound improvement in their body composition (see table 2.2).

Both of these studies revealed a 1.5 pound weekly improvement in body composition resulting from a combination of strength exercise, endurance exercise, and a low-fat nutrition plan. Clearly,

Table 2.1 Changes in body weight, fat, muscle, and body composition for participants who performed strength and endurance exercise with dieting versus participants who performed endurance exercise with dieting (72 subjects)

Exercise program	Body weight change	Fat weight change	Muscle weight change	Body composition change
Strength and endurance (n = 50)	−8.0 lbs.	−10.0 lbs.	+2.0 lbs.	12.0 lbs.
Endurance only (n = 22)	−4.0 lbs.	−4.0 lbs.	0 lbs.	4.0 lbs.

Table 2.2 Changes in body weight, fat, muscle, and body composition for participants who performed strength and endurance exercise with dieting (90 subjects)

Exercise program	Body weight change	Fat weight change	Muscle weight change	Body composition change
Strength and endurance	−6.0 lbs.	−9.5 lbs.	+3.5 lbs.	13.0 lbs.

strength exercise does not hinder fat loss. In fact, strength exercise enhances fat loss by increasing our metabolic requirements for new muscle maintenance.

Athletic Power

Successful sports performance is largely dependent upon the athlete's ability to produce power. Almost every athletic event has a power component. Power is most evident in activities such as putting a shot, punting a football, hitting a baseball, and sprinting 100 yards. But power is also involved in swimming one mile, running five miles, and cycling 25 miles.

In simplest terms, power is the combination of two factors: movement speed and movement force. Generally speaking, we can improve our performance power by increasing our movement speed, increasing our movement force, or both. Our movement speed is specific to each athletic activity and is best improved through high-quality skill training. Our movement force is dependent upon our muscle strength and is best improved through high-quality strength training. Although both power components are important for peak sports performance, it is better to practice each component separately—skill training to develop greater movement speed and strength training to develop greater movement force.

Consider how strength training may benefit a technical athletic skill such as driving a golf ball. The golfer may gain distance by swinging the club faster but may lose control in the process. The golfer may also gain distance by swinging the club with greater muscle force. In this manner, the golfer may increase driving distance while maintaining striking accuracy because the basic swinging movement is not altered.

It should be noted that increased muscle strength does not hinder our movement speed or flexibility. In fact, properly performed strength training may enhance our flexibility by alternately stressing and stretching opposing muscle groups through a full range of movement.

Several years ago, athletes were typically advised to avoid strength exercise. Today, most professional, college, and high school athletic teams utilize strength specialists to design balanced strength-training programs that develop strong athletes and reduce the risk of sports injuries. Sensible strength training certainly contributes to improved athletic performance.

Injury Prevention

The body, like an automobile, needs shock absorbers to prevent potential injuries from external forces. It also requires balancing agents to prevent potential injuries from internal forces. A well-conditioned and well-balanced muscular system serves both of these functions.

One of the best reasons for participating in a strength-training program is to reduce the risk of common injuries. Since World War II, progressive resistance exercise has been the preferred method of injury rehabilitation. It is now understood that proper strength training may be equally useful for injury prevention.

A strong muscular system offers some protection against impact injuries, such as those caused by collision sports or running/jumping activities. For example, high-impact aerobics classes subject the ankles, knees, hips, and back to repetitive landing forces leading to a high rate of joint injuries. Well-conditioned muscles absorb more of the impact forces, thereby reducing stress on the joint structures.

A balanced musculoskeletal system is equally important for preventing over-use injuries. These injuries often result from doing too much work with some muscle groups and too little work with the opposing muscle groups. For example, distance runners frequently encounter overuse injuries to their knee joints. Part of the problem is that distance running overstresses the rear leg muscles and under-emphasizes the front leg muscles. This creates a front-to-back muscle imbalance that decreases knee joint stability and increases the risk of injury.

Although solutions are seldom simple, a first step is balanced strength exercise for all of the major muscle groups. When all of the muscles are strong, there is considerably less chance of one muscle group overpowering another and causing overuse injuries.

Of course, running is not unique. Every athletic event stresses some muscle groups more than others, which sets the stage for overuse injuries. All athletes should therefore perform regular strength training to maintain muscle balance, prevent overuse injuries, and improve sports performance.

Athletes are not the only people who encounter musculoskeletal injuries. Four out of every five Americans experience low-back difficulties, most of which result from muscle weakness or muscle imbalance. Because 80 percent of low-back problems are muscular in nature, sensible strength training may help prevent this common and chronic problem.

Properly performed strength exercise can increase muscle strength, improve muscle balance, and reduce injury potential. However, it should be understood that improperly performed strength exercise can be the cause of injury. Chapter 6 presents important guidelines for designing safe and effective strength-training programs.

Personal Appearance

Continuing the automobile analogy, our muscles are also similar to the chassis of a car. That is, they are largely responsible for our overall personal appearance. In fact, the main reason many people begin a strength-training program is to look better. Looking fit is mostly a matter of muscle conditioning. Strength exercise stimulates our muscle fibers to increase in size and strength, thereby enhancing our muscle appearance and firmness.

Consider the thousands of men and women who have participated in strength-training programs during the past decade. Most have experienced favorable improvements in muscle size, muscle strength, and personal appearance, but few have developed unusually large muscles. This may explain why strength training is becoming one of the most popular physical activities among adults.

Take a typical young woman who weighs 130 pounds and is 26 percent body fat. If she loses four pounds of fat and gains four pounds of muscle, she will still weigh 130 pounds but will be only 23 percent body fat. Although she could lose four pounds of fat through diet and endurance exercise, the best way to add four pounds of muscle is through strength training. It is the four pounds of additional muscle that produces the greatest improvement in her personal appearance.

Strength training is unique in that the positive physical changes are readily apparent to the exerciser and to others. Improvements in body composition are usually noticeable after four to eight weeks of training, and these visible benefits provide excellent motivation to continue strength training.

Self-Satisfaction

Contrary to advertisements in popular muscle magazines, few people who practice strength training develop championship physiques. Simply stated, the capacity to attain really large muscles depends on favorable genetic factors that few of us possess. However, everyone has the potential to look better, feel better, and function better as a result of intelligent strength training. This alone has a major impact on our self-satisfaction index. Studies with youth, teens, adults, and seniors all indicate a higher level of self-satisfaction subsequent to a successful strength-training program. Both the exercise process and the training product provide positive reinforcement to the participant.

Other Benefits

In addition to these important strength-training outcomes, other beneficial physiological adaptations have been identified. These include reduced blood pressure, improved blood cholesterol profile, better glucose metabolism, and increased bone-mineral density.

As presented in this chapter, strength exercise is an excellent means for developing our physical capacity, increasing our metabolic function, improving our athletic power, reducing our injury risk, enhancing our personal appearance, and raising our self-satisfaction level. Remember that our muscles serve as the engine, shock absorbers, and chassis of our body. For most of us, the potential for muscular improvement is high, and the benefits of strength fitness are too important to be taken lightly.

Three

Strength Potential

Our strength potential is related to several factors, many of which are genetic in nature and are generally unchangeable. These essentially fixed characteristics include age, gender, somatotype, muscle length, muscle fiber type, and tendon insertion point. Other aspects of achieving our strength potential involve training experience, training technique, and training specificity. These are performance factors over which we do have control, and it is important to address these variables when designing and evaluating our personal strength-training program.

Age

Males and females increase their muscle size and strength through the process of growth and maturation until about age 20. However, unless they engage in regular strength training, their muscle size and strength gradually decrease throughout adulthood. Fortunately, it is possible to add muscle mass at any age through progressive-resistance exercise.

Consider the results of a research study in which 81 youth (boys and girls) and 282 adults (men and women) performed about 20 minutes of strength exercise, three days a week for eight weeks. As shown in figure 3.1, the youth added four pounds of muscle (lean tissue), and the adults gained three pounds of muscle.

Because of the recent interest in senior fitness, a follow-up study was conducted with 68 older men and women (average age 65 years), and showed a three-pound muscle increase after eight

15

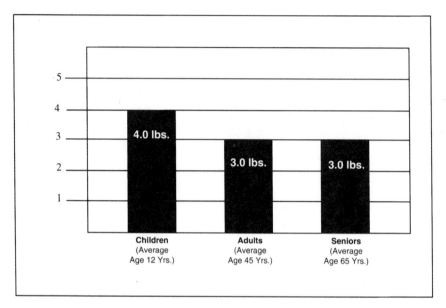

Figure 3.1 Muscle gains after two months of strength training in three age groups (431 subjects)

weeks of training (see figure 3.1). The relatively large improvement may have been due to the seniors' greater potential for replacing muscle that had been lost during the aging process.

Gender

Regarding muscle size and strength, there are definite differences between men and women. During the adolescent growth years, males develop larger muscles than females, which provides a significant strength advantage. Furthermore, strength training increases muscle size to a greater degree in males than in females. This is due to the male sex hormone testosterone, which plays a major role in muscle growth and hypertrophy.

By virtue of their genetic makeup, males generally have greater potential for muscle size and strength than females. Nonetheless, on a pound-for-pound basis, there is little strength difference between males and females.

In one research study, over 900 men and women were evaluated for quadriceps muscle strength on a Nautilus leg extension machine. As shown in table 3.1, the men lifted about 50 percent more weight than the women. When adjusted for size differences, the men performed 10 repetitions with 62 percent of their bodyweight, and the women performed 10 repetitions with 55 percent of their body weight. When further adjusted for fat differences, the men performed 10 repetitions with 74 percent of their lean bodyweight, and the women performed 10 repetitions with 73 percent of their lean bodyweight (See appendix A for strength test protocol and evaluation criteria).

It would therefore appear that men are stronger than women due to muscle quantity, not muscle quality. Men simply have more muscle mass than women and therefore have a higher strength potential.

In terms of strength development, men and women progress at about the same rate. Several research studies have revealed strength gains between 3 and 9 percent per week for both males and females involved in similar strength-training programs. Figure 3.2 illustrates the rate of strength development for male and female subjects during five weeks of a strength-training program.

Somatotype

Generally speaking, there are three basic physique patterns, sometimes referred to as light, medium, or heavy frames (see figure 3.3). More specifically, these physique patterns are called somatotypes. At one extreme are ectomorphs. These individuals are characterized by a linear appearance due to relatively low levels of muscle and fat (see figure 3.4).

At the other extreme are endomorphs. These individuals are characterized by a round appearance due to relatively high levels of fat. As shown in figure 3.4, some endomorphs have lower levels of muscle while others have higher levels of muscle.

Mesomorphs fall between ectomorphs and endomorphs in frame type. Mesomorphic individuals are characterized by a block-like appearance due to relatively high levels of muscle and low levels of fat (see figure 3.4). Because mesomorphs are naturally

Table 3.1 Quadriceps strength for men and women as measured by the 10-repetition maximum weightload on a Nautilus leg extension machine (907 subjects)

	Men	Women
Age	43 yrs.	42 yrs.
Bodyweight	191 lbs.	143 lbs.
10-Rep max	119 lbs.	79 lbs.
Strength quotient (bodyweight)	62%	55%
Strength quotient (lean bodyweight)	74%	73%

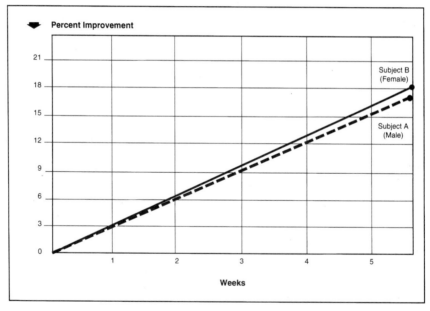

Figure 3.2 Increase in bench press strength as indicated by percent improvement (Bodyweights: male = 160 lbs; female = 95 lbs.)

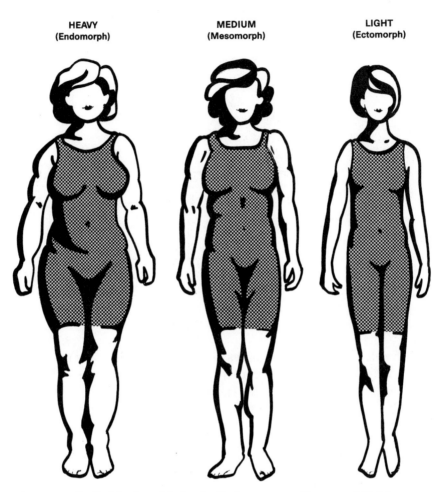

Figure 3.3 Individuals with basically heavy, medium, and light frames

muscular, they respond most favorably to strength exercise and are best suited for bodybuilding programs. However, strength training can increase muscle size to some degree in all body types.

The cross-sectional size of a muscle largely determines the amount of force it can produce. In general, a square centimeter of muscle tissue can produce from two to four pounds of contraction force. It therefore stands to reason that as a muscle becomes larger it also becomes stronger.

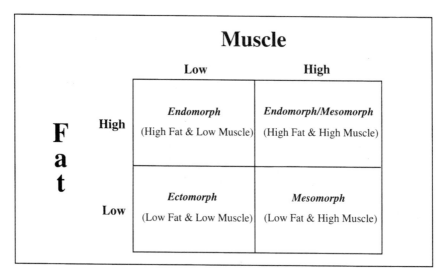

Figure 3.4 Relative amounts of muscle and fat for ectomorphic, endomorphic, and mesomorphic individuals

Strength exercise stimulates individual muscle fibers to enlarge by increasing their protein content. The gradual increase in muscle size that results from strength training is called hypertrophy. Conversely, the gradual decrease in muscle size that occurs when strength training is discontinued is known as atrophy.

Muscle Length

Our potential for muscle size is closely related to our relative muscle length. As illustrated in figures 3.5a and b, some people have short muscles with long tendon attachments. Relatively short muscles have less potential for attaining large size and strength.

Other individuals have long muscles with short tendon attachments (see figures 3.5a and b). Relatively long muscles have more potential for attaining large size and strength.

Most of us inherit medium-length muscles and have moderate potential for increasing our muscle size and strength (see figures 3.5a and b). A simple method for estimating your relative muscle length is presented in appendix B.

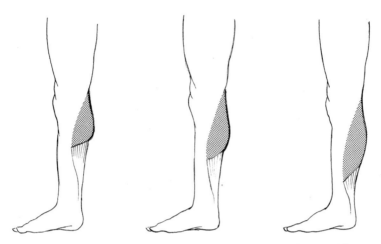

Figure 3.5a Comparison of short, medium, and long calf muscles

Figure 3.5b Comparison of short, medium, and long biceps muscles

Muscle Fiber Type

Our muscle fiber type is another important factor impacting on strength performance. Individual muscle fibers basically possess either slow-twitch (Type I) or fast-twitch (Type II) characteristics.

Slow-twitch muscle fibers bear the greatest burden in aerobic activities that require long periods of relatively low force production. These fibers are smaller and better-suited for aerobic energy utilization. Persons who inherit a high percentage of slow-twitch muscle fibers typically excel as long-distance runners, cyclists, and swimmers.

Fast-twitch muscle fibers bear the greatest burden in anaerobic activities that require short periods of relatively high force production. These fibers are larger and better suited for anaerobic energy utilization. Persons who inherit a high percentage of fast-twitch muscle fibers typically excel as sprinters, jumpers, and throwers.

Individuals with mostly fast-twitch muscle fibers have greater potential for increasing muscle size and strength than individuals with mostly slow-twitch muscle fibers. Most of us inherit a fairly even mix of fast-twitch and slow-twitch muscle fibers, and have moderate potential for increasing our muscle size and strength. A method for estimating your muscle fiber type is presented in appendix C.

Tendon Insertion Point

Human movement is dependent upon a system of levers involving the bones, joints, and muscles. Muscles connect to bones by means of tendon attachments. Figure 3.6 shows two identical upper arm bones, lower arm bones, and biceps muscles. However, the biceps tendon on the left attaches three-quarters of an inch from the elbow and the biceps tendon on the right attaches one inch from the elbow. This results in a leverage advantage for the biceps muscle on the right.

Let's say that in both cases the biceps muscle produces 200 pounds of force and that the forearm is 10 inches in length. Using the following formula, we find a major difference in functional force output.

Muscle Force × Force Arm = Resistance Force × Resistance Arm

> Example on left (fig. 3.6)
> 200 pounds × ¾ inch = 15 pounds × 10 inches
> Functional force output = 15 pounds
>
> Example on right (fig. 3.6)
> 200 pounds × 1 inch = 20 pounds × 10 inches
> Functional force output = 20 pounds

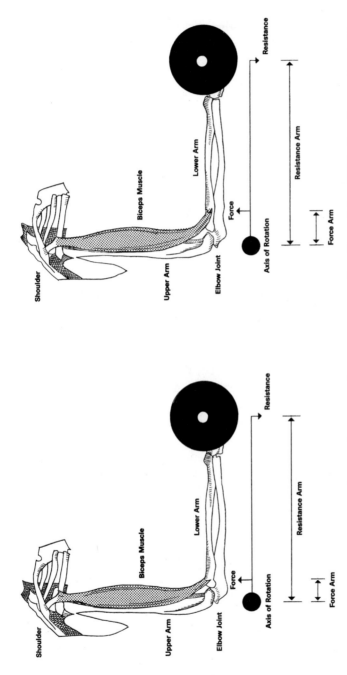

Figure 3.6 The biceps muscle attaches to the lower arm near the elbow joint. With the elbow at a right angle, the muscle force times the force arm equals the resistance times the resistance arm. The biceps on the left attaches closer to the elbow joint (less force output), the biceps on the right attaches farther from the elbow joint (more force output).

These examples demonstrate two points. First, human leverage systems require large amounts of muscle force to overcome small amounts of resistance force. Second, small differences in tendon insertion points may produce large differences in functional force output. Although there is no simple means for determining one's tendon insertion point, persons who are stronger than they appear are likely to have more favorable tendon attachments.

Training Experience

Training experience refers to the length of time you have been involved in a strength-training program. Clearly, the person who has trained consistently for three years will make smaller strength gains than the person who has trained for only three weeks. During the early stages of a strength-training program, improvement is both rapid and substantial due to learning processes. As you approach your strength potential, increases come more slowly and in smaller increments.

As illustrated in figure 3.7, the rate of strength development may decrease considerably during the first three months of training. For example, a 40 percent strength gain may be experienced during the first month of exercise. However, the strength increase may be limited to 10 percent during the second month, and only 2.5 percent during the third month.

Experienced strength trainers tend to encounter strength plateaus, when further progress seems unlikely. However, with appropriate changes in your exercise routine, you can continue to make performance improvements and maintain your training motivation. Chapter 9 discusses strength plateaus in more detail, and presents several strategies for advancing beyond temporary limitations.

Training Technique

Your training technique may have a profound influence on both your strength development and your injury risk. For example, when you use fast movement speed you may curl 100 pounds for 10 repetitions. This training technique is characterized by high

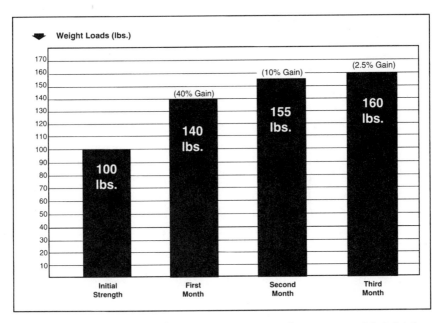

Figure 3.7 Sample three-month improvement for person with initial leg extension weightload of 100 pounds

muscle force at the beginning of each lift and low muscle force thereafter. Although there is some stimulus to your biceps, most of the force comes from assisting muscle groups and momentum. Consequently, there is more stress on your joint structures and a high risk of tissue injury.

When you use slow movement speed you may curl 75 pounds for 10 repetitions. This training technique is characterized by consistent muscle force throughout the movement range. Although less weight is used, most of the force comes from the biceps which provides an excellent strength stimulus for this muscle group. Equally important, there is less stress on your joint structures and a low risk of tissue injury.

Fast lifting movements emphasize assisting muscles and momentum, thereby decreasing the training effect and increasing the injury potential. Slow lifting movements emphasize the target muscles and de-emphasize momentum, thereby increasing the training effect and decreasing the injury potential.

Proper training technique is the key to successful strength development. Make every repetition count by lifting and lowering the resistance in a slow and controlled manner throughout the full movement range.

Training Specificity

People frequently equate hard work with success, but this is only true when there is a strong relationship between the work performed and the desired outcomes. Both a one-hour run and a one-hour weight-training session are hard work, but each produces a specific physical response. A serious distance runner and a serious weight lifter may train over an hour each day, but their physical appearances are very different.

Training that involves long periods of low-intensity exercise may develop cardiovascular endurance but may not improve muscle strength. Conversely, training that involves short periods of high-intensity exercise may develop muscle strength but may not improve cardiovascular endurance.

You should therefore train in a specific manner to obtain specific results: strength training for muscular development and endurance training for cardiovascular development. Figure 3.8 indicates the approximate positions of various physical activities along the strength–endurance continuum. Note that strength-related exercise is of high intensity and short duration, whereas endurance-related exercise is of low intensity and long duration.

Strength is best developed by working within the anaerobic energy system. The anaerobic energy system may be best stressed by performing about 50 to 70 seconds of high-effort exercise. This may be best accomplished through 8 to 12 controlled repetitions to the point of momentary muscle failure. This important training concept will be addressed in more detail in chapter 6.

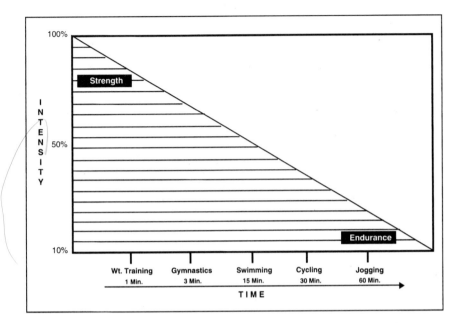

Figure 3.8 Position of various activities along the strength-endurance continuum. Note that strength-related activities are of relatively high intensity and short duration.

Four

Muscle Physiology

While you can certainly gain strength without understanding exactly how a muscle produces force, the more you know about muscle structure and function, the better. How your muscles respond to resistance exercise is important information that will help you attain greater strength gains.

In simplest terms, sensible strength training provides the stimulus for muscle growth. Specifically, muscles respond to progressive stress by increasing their protein content and developing larger fibers. This produces larger muscles that have greater strength capacity and higher energy requirements.

Muscle Structure

The protein components that give muscle the ability to produce force are known as filaments. As shown in figure 4.1, there are thick protein strands, called myosin filaments, and thin protein strands, called actin filaments. Small extensions of the myosin filaments, known as cross-bridges, permit the myosin filaments to connect with the actin filaments in a mechanical interaction.

Each section of the actin-myosin complex is called a sarcomere, and serves as the smallest functional unit of muscle contraction. Upon electrical stimulation from a motor nerve, the thin actin filaments are pulled toward the thick myosin filaments, causing the muscle to shorten (see figure 4.2).

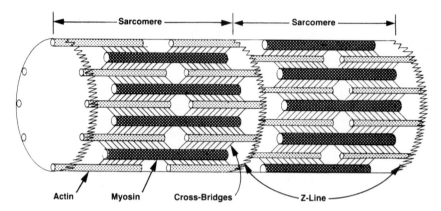

Figure 4.1 The smallest functional unit of muscle contraction, the sarcomere, consists of thin actin filaments, thick myosin filaments, and tiny cross-bridges that serve as coupling agents between the myosin proteins and the surrounding actin proteins.

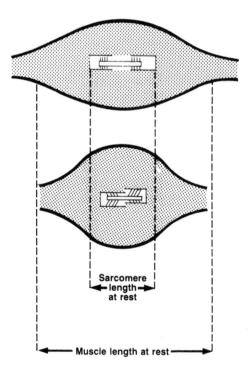

Figure 4.2 Changes in length of individual sarcomeres and entire muscle during concentric muscle contraction

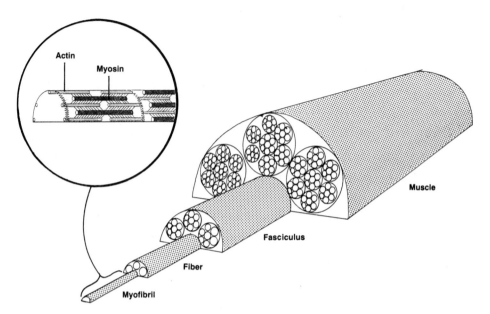

Figure 4.3 The structural and functional components of skeletal muscle

The actin and myosin filaments form myofibrils, which are the principle threads running throughout the muscles. As illustrated in figure 4.3, groups of myofibrils are bound together into individual muscle fibers. In turn, muscle fibers are bound together into larger units known as fiber bundles. The fiber bundles are enclosed by a sheath of connective tissue and function together as a muscle, such as the biceps.

Muscle Function

Muscle function is essentially dependent upon three factors: electrical stimulus, chemical energy, and mechanical interaction.

Electrical Stimulus

Each muscle fiber has a threshold level of electrical stimulus necessary to initiate the contraction process. When the required level of electrical stimulus is received, the muscle fiber contracts with maximum force. This is known as the all-or-none law of muscle contraction. If the electrical stimulus is below threshold level, the muscle fiber does not contract. If the electrical stimulus is above threshold level, the muscle fiber contracts 100 percent. It is not possible for a muscle fiber to produce intermediate levels of force.

Chemical Energy

For the contraction process to occur, there must be a sufficient source of available energy. The basic energy source for muscle function is called adenosine triphosphate, or ATP. These high-energy phosphates are available within our muscles, but they are depleted quickly during maximum effort exercise. Once depleted, the ATP stores must be replenished for muscle contraction to continue.

For example, following a set of biceps curls to momentary muscle failure, it is necessary to rest temporarily before attempting a second set. A two-minute rest/recovery period is adequate to replenish over 90 percent of the muscle's ATP stores (see appendix D).

Mechanical Interaction

Given sufficient electrical stimulus and chemical energy, the actin and myosin filaments engage in mechanical interaction that causes the muscle fiber to shorten. This mechanical interaction process, known as the sliding filament theory of muscle contraction, is responsible for muscle force production.

Muscle Relaxation

The natural state of skeletal muscle is called relaxation. Muscle fibers contract only upon receiving appropriate nerve stimulation. In the absence of an electrical stimulus, the contraction process is inactive, muscle force is not developed, and the muscle is relaxed.

Muscle contraction and muscle relaxation occur simultaneously during most movements. For example, during a biceps curl, the biceps muscles are stimulated to contract and shorten. At the same time, the opposing triceps muscles are cued to relax and lengthen. Actually, the degree of tension and relaxation in our opposing muscle groups is precisely regulated by our nervous system to produce smooth movements with varying degrees of force and speed.

Muscle Contraction

When a muscle is activated, it produces tension and attempts to shorten. That is, it tries to pull its attachments closer together. However, a contracting muscle may actually shorten, lengthen, or remain the same size, depending upon the force–resistance relationship.

Positive Contraction

When a barbell is lifted from the hip to the shoulder during the upward phase of the standing curl exercise, the biceps muscles exert force, shorten, and overcome the resistance (see figure 4.4a). Whenever muscles do this, they are said to contract positively or concentrically. Positive muscle contractions are essential for overcoming the force of gravity and performing lifting movements.

Negative Contraction

When a barbell is lowered from the shoulder to the hip during the downward phase of the standing curl exercise, the biceps muscles exert force, lengthen, and are overcome by the resistance (see figure 4.4b). Whenever muscles do this, they are said to contract negatively or eccentrically. Negative muscle contractions are essential for reducing the force of gravity and performing controlled lowering movements. Note that if the biceps muscles did not exert force during the downward phase of the standing curl exercise, the barbell would drop in a quick, uncontrolled, and dangerous manner.

Static Contraction

When a barbell is held at the midpoint of the standing curl exercise, the biceps muscles exert force but do not change in length. They neither overcome the resistance nor are they overcome by the

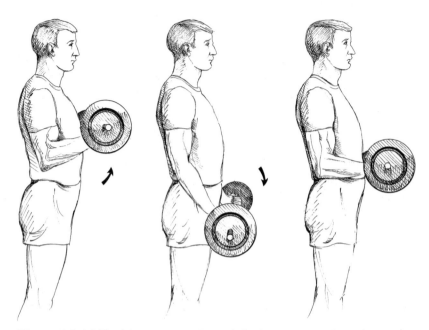

Figure 4.4 (a) Positive contraction of the biceps muscles lifting an 80-pound barbell. (b) Negative contraction of the biceps muscles lowering a 120-pound barbell. (c) Static contraction of the biceps muscles holding a 100-pound barbell

resistance (see figure 4.4c). Whenever a muscle exerts force but does not change in length, it is said to contract statically or isometrically. Static muscle contractions are essential for matching the force of gravity and maintaining given joint positions.

Muscle Force Output

Muscle force output is most accurately measured during a static contraction, because no movement is involved. Whenever a muscle shortens, internal friction decreases the effective force output. Conversely, whenever a muscle lengthens, internal friction increases the effective force output. This is due to the fact that friction always works against the direction of movement.

For example, Mark can hold (static contraction) a 100-pound barbell at a right angle, as illustrated in figure 4.4c. He can slowly lift (positive contraction) an 80-pound barbell, as illustrated in figure 4.4a; or he can slowly lower (negative contraction) a 120-pound barbell, as illustrated in figure 4.4b. In each case, Mark's muscle force production is 100 pounds. However, internal muscle friction decreases his positive force output by about 20 percent and increases his negative force output by about 20 percent. These differences in muscle force output have important implications for sensible strength training. For example, you may not be able to lift your body to the chin-up bar (positive contraction), but you can probably lower your body from the chin-up bar (negative contraction).

Prime Mover Muscles

In any given joint action, the muscle that is principally responsible for controlling the movement is termed the prime mover muscle. The prime mover muscle contracts positively when lifting a weight and negatively when lowering a weight. As an example, the biceps are the prime mover muscles for standing curls, both lifting and lowering.

Many exercises involve more than one prime mover muscle group. Chin-ups, for example, involve the biceps muscles of the arms and the latissimus dorsi muscles of the back. Both of these prime mover muscle groups are activated during the lifting and lowering phase of chin-ups.

Antagonist Muscles

The muscle that produces the opposite movement of the prime mover is called the antagonist. For example, the triceps muscles are the antagonists of the biceps muscles. For smooth joint movements, the prime mover muscles contract and shorten as the antagonist muscles relax and lengthen. In the case of standing curls, the biceps muscles contract and shorten as the triceps muscles relax and lengthen.

Stabilizer Muscles

For the desired movements to occur in certain joints, other joints must be stabilized. For example, to properly perform standing curls, the torso must remain erect and the upper arms must be held against the sides. The torso is stabilized by static contraction of the low-back muscles, and the upper arms are stabilized by static contraction of the chest and upper-back muscles.

A similar torso stabilization must occur to properly perform push-ups. The midsection muscles must contract statically to maintain the body in a straight and stable position. The muscles that perform stabilizing functions are referred to as stabilizer muscles.

Motor Unit

Muscle contraction is regulated by the motor unit. A motor unit is made up of a single motor neuron and all the muscle fibers that receive stimulation from that nerve (see figure 4.5). In large muscles, such as the rectus femoris, a single motor neuron may innervate several hundred muscle fibers. In smaller muscles, such as those that produce precise movements of the eyes, each motor neuron may innervate only a few muscle fibers. In all cases, all of the muscle fibers in a given motor unit contract with maximum force when activated.

Motor unit recruitment is the key to smooth, forceful, and sustained muscle contraction. Because the muscle fibers in a given motor unit are distributed throughout the muscle, only a few motor units need to be activated for coordinated muscle contraction. This arrangement allows individual motor units to alternately fire and rest when work is performed at submaximal strength levels.

Because muscles are required to exert varying degrees of force (e.g., placing a light bulb in an overhead socket versus pressing a 90-pound barbell), some type of regulatory system is essential. There are two factors that affect the strength of a muscle contraction. These are the frequency of nerve impulses and the number of motor units activated. Fine adjustments in muscle tension are produced by changes in the frequency of nerve impulses to the muscle fibers. As the frequency of nerve impulses increases, the strength of contraction increases; and as the frequency of nerve impulses decreases, the

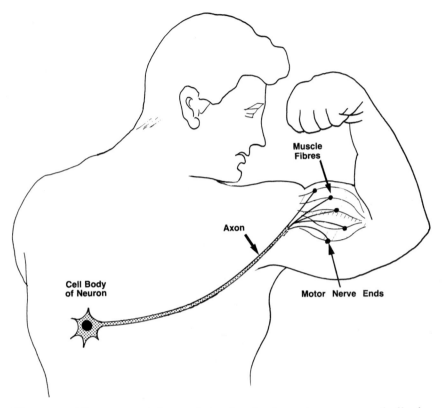

Figure 4.5 The motor unit consists of a single motor nerve and all of the muscle fibers that it innervates.

strength of contraction decreases. Gross variations in muscle tension are dependent upon the number of motor units activated by the central nervous system. The more motor units recruited, the stronger the muscle contraction and vice versa. Under normal circumstances, different motor units fire independently. When maximum strength is required, nerve impulses may arrive more synchronously, thus enabling the muscle to produce greater tension.

Fiber Types

Although the strength of contraction in skeletal muscles is primarily regulated by our central nervous system, the individual motor units possess different contractile capacities, generally referred to as slow-twitch (Type I) or fast-twitch (Type II) characteristics. Slow-twitch muscle fibers produce less force for longer duration, whereas fast-twitch muscle fibers produce more force for shorter duration. These differences are due to both the fiber size and physiological factors.

Slow-twitch muscle fibers are smaller and better suited for aerobic energy utilization because they contain more mitochondria, more endurance enzymes, more blood capillaries, and more intramuscular triglyceride stores. Fast-twitch muscle fibers are larger and better suited for anaerobic energy utilization because they have more glycolytic enzymes and more intramuscular phosphate stores. Fast-twitch fibers also contain more contractile proteins and hypertrophy to a greater degree in response to resistance exercise.

Research indicates that both slow-twitch motor units and fast-twitch motor units are recruited for maximum force production. When submaximum efforts are required, slow-twitch motor units are activated first, followed by fast-twitch motor units if necessary.

It is unlikely that we can change our proportion of slow-twitch and fast-twitch muscle fibers through strength exercise. However, it may be possible to enhance the endurance of our fast-twitch muscle fibers through specialized training.

Fiber Arrangement

Another factor that influences the strength of contraction is the muscle fiber arrangement. There are basically two types of fiber patterns, fusiform and penniform. Fusiform muscles have long fibers that run parallel to the line of pull. Muscles of this type produce less force but have a large range of movement. The biceps femoris muscle of the hamstrings group is fusiform. Penniform muscles have short fibers that run diagonally to the line of pull. Penniform muscles, therefore, produce greater force but have s smaller range of movement. Figure 4.6 presents schematic drawings of a fusiform muscle and two types of penniform muscles—penniform unipennate and the stronger penniform bipennate. The semitendinosus muscle of the hamstrings group is penniform unipennate, and the rectus femoris muscle of the quadriceps group is penniform bipennate.

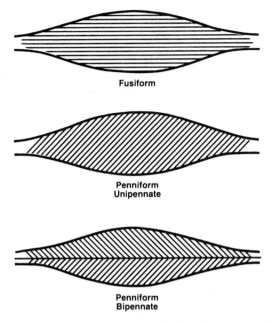

Figure 4.6 Schematic representations of a fusiform muscle, a unipennate muscle, and a bipennate muscle

Muscle Protection

Our bodies are equipped with built-in mechanisms to prevent tissue damage as a result of either too much muscle force or too much muscle stretch. Golgi tendon organs are located within our muscle tendons. When we produce dangerously high levels of force, the Golgi tendon organs act to inhibit further muscle contraction, thereby reducing the risk of injury.

Muscle spindles are located within our muscles. When a muscle is stretched too quickly, the muscle spindles trigger a reflex action that causes the muscle to contract, thereby preventing it from being overstretched to the point of injury.

Muscle Fatigue

The exact mechanisms responsible for muscle fatigue are not fully understood. However, exercise physiologists have identified several potential fatigue sites, including the central nervous system, the motor nerve, the neuromuscular junction, and the contractile mechanism itself.

Basically, as a muscle continues to contract against high resistance, the anaerobic energy source (ATP) becomes temporarily depleted. At the same time, anaerobic by-products such as lactic acid accumulate in the muscle. This increases tissue acidity, which adversely affects contractile ability. In addition to these factors, chemical changes at the nerve–muscle junction may hinder further muscle contraction.

Muscle fatigue may be experienced in varying degrees. At the point of temporary muscle failure, the muscle is no longer capable of positive contraction and the exercise set is typically terminated. After a few seconds rest, the muscle's contraction ability is partially restored, and after two minutes of recovery, the anaerobic energy source is essentially replaced.

The immediate effect of exercising to the point of momentary muscle failure is varying degrees of discomfort, including muscle tightness and a localized burning sensation. Fortunately, the muscle discomfort felt during and immediately after the exercise set passes quickly.

Muscle Soreness

A more sustained muscle ache may be experienced a day or two after your strength workout. This is referred to as delayed-onset muscle soreness. Many exercise physiologists believe that delayed-onset muscle soreness is due to tissue microtrauma resulting from heavy-resistance exercise. These microscopic tears in the muscle and/or connective tissue require a few days for repair and building processes, including protein synthesis leading to larger and stronger muscles. Research indicates that negative muscle contractions produce more muscle microtrauma than positive or isometric muscle contractions. This may be the principal cause of delayed-onset muscle soreness.

Isometric Exercise

Isometric exercise involves static muscle contractions against a resistance. Although there is no movement, the target muscles do develop tension and exert force. Isometric exercise is effective for increasing muscle strength, but it has a few notable drawbacks.

First, isometric strength gains are quite specific to the joint positions that are trained, with relatively little strength improvement in other joint positions. It is therefore necessary to train at several points in the movement range for overall strength development.

Second, isometric exercise is characterized by tightly contracted muscles that occlude blood flow and trigger large increases in blood pressure. This factor is of particular significance to persons with cardiovascular problems or blood pressure concerns.

Third, it is difficult to assess accurately the training effort and strength improvement associated with most types of isometric exercise. The lack of movement makes isometric exercise monotonous for many people who prefer to see weights moving as a result of their muscular effort.

Isokinetic Exercise

Isokinetic exercise is performed on equipment that provides a constant movement speed and that varies the resistance force in accordance with your muscle force. In other words, when you apply more muscle force you encounter more resistance force, and when you apply less muscle force you encounter less resistance force. Most isokinetic machines offer resistance only during positive (concentric) contractions.

There are two key factors in isokinetic exercise. First, the movement speed remains the same throughout each repetition. Second, your muscle force determines the resistance force.

Isotonic Exercise

Isotonic exercise is essentially the opposite of isokinetic exercise. First, the movement speed does not necessarily remain the same throughout each repetition. Second, the resistance force determines your muscle force. That is, when you use more resistance force you produce more muscle force, and when you use less resistance force you produce less muscle force. Isotonic exercise offers resistance during both positive (concentric) and negative (eccentric) contractions.

Dynamic-constant Resistance Exercise

One form of isotonic exercise is known as dynamic-constant resistance exercise. As the name implies, you lift and lower a constant resistance through a particular movement range. Although the actual resistance does not vary (e.g., a 20-pound dumbbell), both the resistance force and your muscle force change considerably throughout the movement range due to leverage factors. That is, for a given movement, the resistance force is higher in some positions than others, and your muscle force is higher in some positions than others. Consequently, your muscle force and the resistance force may not be closely matched throughout much of the exercise movement.

Dynamic-variable Resistance Exercise

To better match muscle force and resistance force throughout the movement range, many types of strength-training equipment incorporate dynamic-variable resistance exercise. Through the use of levers, cams, or linkage systems, these machines automatically change the resistance in accordance with your muscle force capacity. That is, the equipment provides more resistance in positions of higher muscle force capacity and less resistance in positions of lower muscle force capacity.

Dynamic-constant resistance exercise and dynamic-variable resistance exercise are both effective for developing muscle strength. Dynamic-variable resistance exercise simply provides a more consistent relationship between your muscle force and the resistance force.

Five

Movement Mechanics

Human movement is more complicated than it may appear. For example, rising from a chair to a standing position requires simultaneous contraction of two opposing muscle groups—the quadriceps and hamstrings. The quadriceps are the prime movers for knee extension and hip flexion, whereas the hamstrings are the prime movers for knee flexion and hip extension.

As illustrated in figure 5.1, leverage factors make it possible for both muscle groups to contract powerfully and productively at the same time. Due to a more favorable tendon insertion point at the knee joint, the quadriceps overpower the hamstrings—resulting in knee extension. Due to a more favorable tendon insertion point at the hip joint, the hamstrings overpower the quadriceps—resulting in hip extension. Thus, these opposing muscle groups work together during co-contraction to produce the desired joint actions and movement mechanics.

Lever Systems

To better understand the nuts and bolts of human movement, it is important to begin with lever systems. Our lever systems are composed of muscles, bones, and joints. Our muscles produce the force to move our bones around our joint axes of rotation.

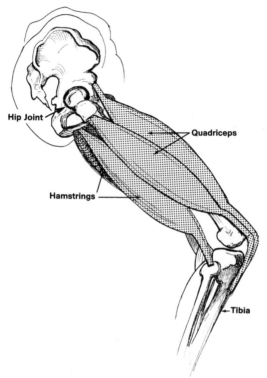

Figure 5.1 The quadriceps attach farther from the knee joint than the hamstrings, providing a leverage advantage for knee extension when both muscles contract simultaneously. The hamstrings attach farther from the hip joint than the quadriceps, providing a leverage advantage for hip extension when both muscles contract simultaneously.

First-class Levers

When our joint axis of rotation is between the muscle force and the resistance force, the system functions as a first-class lever. As shown in figure 5.2, elbow extension is a first-class lever system because the joint axis of rotation (elbow) is between the muscle force (triceps) and the resistance force (weightstack cable). Because the force arm (distance from the muscle insertion to the joint axis) is shorter than the resistance arm (distance from the resistance to the joint axis), our first-class lever systems require relatively high muscle force to overcome relatively low resistance force.

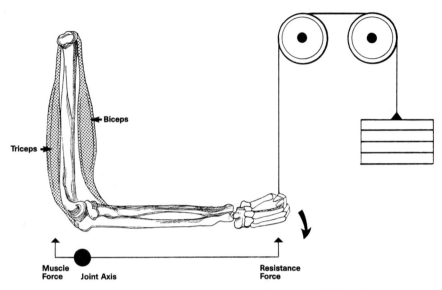

Figure 5.2 First-class lever: the joint axis of rotation (elbow) is between the muscle force (triceps) and the resistance force (weightstack cable).

Second-class Levers

When the resistance force is between our joint axis of rotation and the muscle force, the system operates as a second-class lever. As illustrated in figure 5.3, ankle extension is a second-class lever system because the resistance force (bodyweight) is between the joint axis of rotation (ball of the foot) and the muscle force (gastrocnemius). Because the force arm is longer than the resistance arm, our second-class lever systems require relatively low muscle force to overcome relatively high resistance force.

Third-class Levers

When the muscle force is between our joint axis of rotation and the resistance force, the system functions as a third-class lever. As presented in figure 5.4, elbow flexion is a third-class lever system because the muscle force (biceps) is between the joint axis of rotation (elbow) and the resistance force (dumbbell). Because the force arm is shorter than the resistance arm, our third-class lever systems require relatively high muscle force to overcome relatively low resistance force.

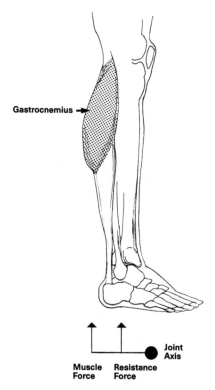

Figure 5.3 Second-class lever: the resistance force (bodyweight) is between the joint axis of rotation (ball of foot) and the muscle force (gastrocnemius).

Basic Joint Movements

Our bodies have almost unlimited movement potential. However, the basic joint movements involve the ankle, knee, hip, trunk, shoulder, elbow, wrist, and neck. Figures 5.5a and 5.5b present the major muscles of the body as viewed from the front and back. Table 5–1 illustrates the basic joint movements, the prime mover muscles, and the specific movement patterns.

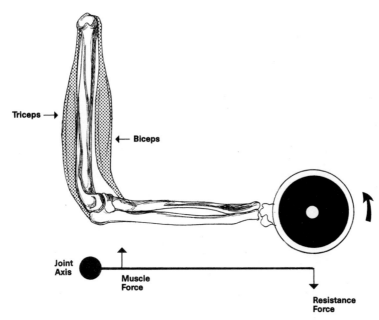

Figure 5.4 Third-class lever: the muscle force (biceps) is between the joint axis of rotation (elbow) and the resistance force (dumbbell).

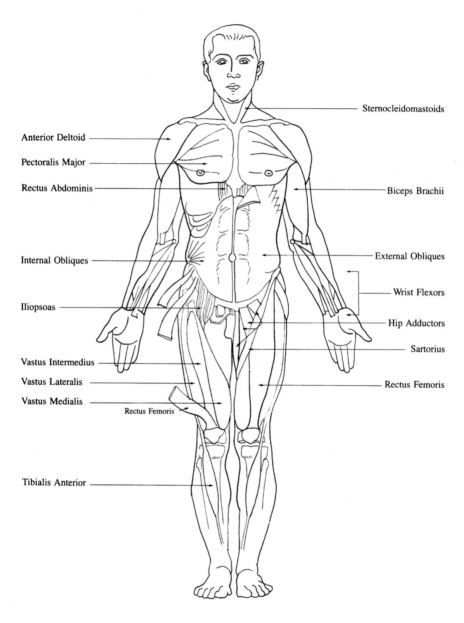

Muscles Front

Figure 5.5a Muscles of the body

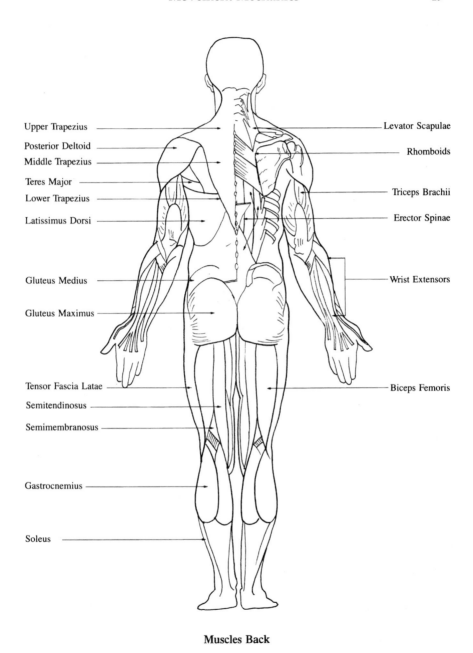

Muscles Back

Figure 5.5b Muscles of the body

Table 5–1 Basic joint movements, illustrated

Joint movement	Prime mover muscles	Specific movement pattern
Ankle extension	Gastrocnemius and soleus	Increasing the angle between the foot and the leg

Joint movement	Prime mover muscles	Specific movement pattern
Ankle flexion	Tibialis anterior	Decreasing the angle between the foot and the leg

Joint movement	Prime mover muscles	Specific movement pattern
Knee extension	Quadriceps group (rectus femoris, vastus lateralis, vastus medialis, and vastus intermedius	Increasing the angle between the thigh and the leg

Joint movement	Prime mover muscles	Specific movement pattern
Knee flexion	Hamstrings group (biceps femoris, semitendinosus, and semimembranosus)	Decreasing the angle between the thigh and the leg

Hip abduction	Abductor group (gluteus medius and tensor fascia latae)	Increasing the angle between the thigh and the midline of the body

Table 5–1   Basic joint movements, illustrated *Continued*

Joint movement	Prime mover muscles	Specific movement pattern
Hip adduction	Adductor group (adductor magnus, adductor longus, adductor brevis, pectineus, and gracilis)	Decreasing the angle between the thigh and the midline of the body

Joint movement	Prime mover muscles	Specific movement pattern
Hip extension	Hamstrings group and gluteus maximus	Increasing the angle between the thigh and the abdomen

Joint movement	Prime mover muscles	Specific movement pattern
Hip flexion	Rectus femoris and iliopsoas	Decreasing the angle between the thigh and the abdomen

Trunk Extension	Erector spinae	Increasing the angle between the chest and the abdomen
Trunk flexion	Rectus abdominis	Decreasing the angle between the chest and the abdomen

Trunk Extension

Trunk Flexion

Table 5–1   Basic joint movements, illustrated *Continued*

Joint movement	Prime mover muscles	Specific movement pattern
Shoulder abduction	Deltoids	Increasing the angle between the arm and the side

Joint movement	Prime mover muscles	Specific movement pattern
Shoulder adduction	Latissimus dorsi, teres major, and pectoralis major	Decreasing the angle between the arm and the side

Joint movement	*Prime mover muscles*	*Specific movement pattern*
Shoulder extension	Latissimus dorsi, teres major, and posterior deltoid	First decreasing, then increasing the angle between the arm and the chest in a backward movement

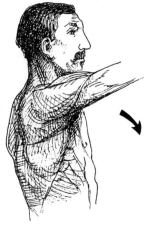

Shoulder flexion	Anterior deltoid	First decreasing, then increasing the angle between the arm and the chest in a forward movement

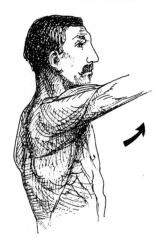

Table 5–1 Basic joint movements, illustrated *Continued*

Joint movement	Prime mover muscles	Specific movement pattern
Shoulder horizontal extension	Posterior deltoid, latissimus dorsi, and teres major	Increasing the angle between the arm and the chest in the horizontal plane

| Shoulder horizontal flexion | Pectoralis major and anterior deltoid | Decreasing the angle between the arm and the chest in the horizontal plane |

Joint movement	Prime mover muscles	Specific movement pattern
Shoulder elevation	Upper trapezius	Decreasing the angle between the shoulders and the neck

Joint movement	Prime mover muscles	Specific movement pattern
Elbow extension	Triceps brachii	Increasing the angle between the arm and the forearm

Table 5–1 Basic joint movements, illustrated *Continued*

Joint movement	Prime mover muscles	Specific movement pattern
Elbow flexion	Biceps brachii	Decreasing the angle between the arm and the forearm

| Wrist extension | Extensor group (extensor carpi ulnaris, extensor digitorum, extensor carpi radialis, and others) | Increasing the angle between the hand and underside of the forearm |

Joint movement	Prime mover muscles	Specific movement pattern
Wrist flexion	Flexor group (flexor carpi ulnaris, palmaris longus, flexor carpi radialis, and others)	Decreasing the angle between the hand and underside of the forearm

| Neck extension | Upper trapezius and levator scapulae | Increasing the angle between the chin and the chest |
| Neck flexion | Sternocleidomastoids | Decreasing the angle between the chin and the chest |

Neck Extension

Neck Flexion

Six

Strength-training Guidelines

The basic principle of strength development is progressive-resistance exercise. That is, the muscle stress gradually increases through a systematic program of heavier workloads.

A crude example of progressive-resistance exercise is provided by the ancient Greek, Milo of Crotona. Legend indicates that Milo carried a bull on his shoulders across the Olympic stadium. He prepared for this strength event by carrying the bull on his shoulders daily from its birth. The growing bull provided an unusual form of progressively heavier resistance.

Although relatively simple in principle, strength exercise may become rather complex in practice. There are many training variables that should be considered when designing a sensible and productive program of strength development.

Bodybuilders, weight lifters, and power athletes typically follow specialized strength-training programs, that will be addressed in chapter 10. The following guidelines for strength exercise are recommended for individuals who desire a safe, effective, and efficient approach to muscular fitness.

Exercise Selection and Order

Chapter 5 identified the basic joint actions and prime mover muscles. It is important to address all of these muscle groups with appropriate resistance exercises.

Training all of our major muscle groups leads to comprehensive strength development, muscle balance, and joint integrity. Conversely, emphasizing some muscle groups over others typically results in fragmented strength development, muscle imbalance, and joint instability—all of which increase injury potential.

It is advisable to train our larger groups first, followed by our medium and smaller muscle groups. It is also prudent to exercise opposing muscle groups in pairs, such as the quadriceps and the hamstrings. However, because the quadriceps are considerably stronger than the hamstrings at the knee joint, you would normally use more resistance in the leg extension exercise than the leg curl exercise.

Practical Application

A sound strength-training program should include exercises for all of our major muscle groups. Proper exercise selection provides balanced muscle development, sets a firm foundation for further improvement, and reduces the risk of overuse injuries. The following chart presents sample muscle-strengthening exercises utilizing both machines and free weights.

Joint movement	Sample machine exercise	Sample free-weight exercise
Ankle extension	—	Barbell heel raise
Ankle flexion	—	Weighted toe raise
Knee extension	Leg extension machine	—
Knee flexion	Leg curl machine	—
Hip abduction	Hip abductor machine	—
Hip adduction	Hip adductor machine	—
Hip extension	Leg press machine	Barbell squat
Hip flexion	—	Hanging knee raise
Trunk extension	Low-back machine	—
Trunk flexion	Abdominal machine	Trunk curl
Shoulder abduction	Lateral raise machine	Dumbbell lateral raise

Joint movement	Sample machine exercise	Sample free-weight exercise
Shoulder adduction	Behind neck machine	Wide grip pull-down
Shoulder extension	Pullover machine	Narrow grip pull-up
Shoulder flexion	—	Dumbbell front raise
Shoulder horizontal extension	Rowing back machine	Dumbbell bent lateral raise
Shoulder horizontal flexion	10-Degree chest machine	Dumbbell bench press
Shoulder elevation	Shoulder shrug machine	Barbell shoulder shrug
Elbow extension	Triceps machine	Dumbbell kickback
Elbow flexion	Biceps machine	Dumbbell curl
Wrist extension	—	Weighted wrist roll
Wrist flexion	—	Weighted wrist roll
Neck extension	Neck machine	—
Neck flexion	Neck machine	—

Exercise Frequency

Muscle development depends upon two equally important training factors. First is progressive-resistance exercise to stress the muscles and stimulate physiological adaptations. Second is sufficient recovery time to permit tissue repair, building, and protein overcompensation leading to larger and stronger muscles.

Muscles become weaker during the exercise session due to tissue microtrauma resulting from heavy-resistance exercise. They become stronger during the period of days following the exercise session. Ideally, our next strength workout should come at the peak of our muscle-building process.

As illustrated in figure 6.1, Jim's leg extension strength is 100 pounds at the beginning of Monday's exercise session, and 90 pounds at the end of Monday's workout. One day later his leg extension strength has recovered to 97.5 pounds, two days later his leg extension strength has reached 102.5 pounds, and three days

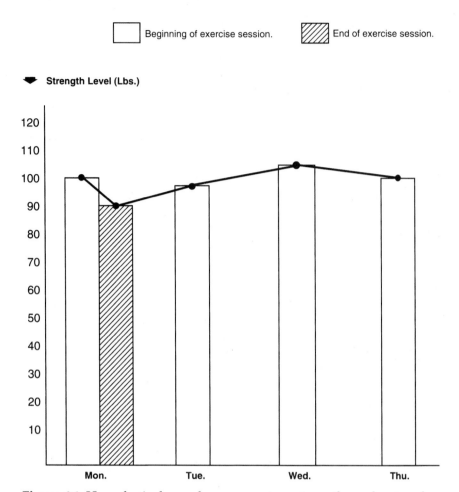

Figure 6.1 Hypothetical muscle response to a strength workout and a three-day recovery period

later his leg extension strength has returned to 100 pounds. In this example, Jim would experience better results by taking his next workout two days after his previous training session.

There are so many genetic, physiological, and psychological factors that affect our muscle-building process, it is impossible to provide specific guidelines in this area. The best advice is to carefully monitor your training response on a day-to-day basis. A well-designed strength-training logbook, such as that presented in

Table 6–1 Effects of different training frequencies on the
development of muscle strength (55 subjects)

Group	(N)	Repetitions per training session	Training sessions per week	Mean percent increase
A	16	60	1	19%
B	20	30	2	17%
C	13	20	3	24%
D	6	12	5	21%

appendix E, should be helpful in this regard. Other things being equal, you should be slightly stronger on successive training sessions when your exercise frequency is appropriate.

One research study (Westcott 1974) found more demanding strength workouts require longer recovery periods, whereas less demanding strength workouts require shorter recovery periods. In an attempt to isolate the frequency variable, total training workloads were equated on a weekly basis. Specifically, all 55 subjects performed 60 repetitions per week with the bench press exercise. As presented in table 6–1, group A trained one day per week (twelve sets of five reps), group B trained two days per week (six sets of five reps), group C trained three days per week (four sets of five reps), and group D trained five days per week (two sets of six reps).

The subjects were tested for maximum bench press strength before and after the 7½ week training period. As shown in table 6–1, all of the training groups made excellent strength gains in the bench press exercise. However, statistical analyses of the data showed no significant differences among the four training groups. These findings indicate that different training frequencies may be acceptable for strength development depending upon the exercise protocols. However, because group D had only six subjects, it may be best not to generalize the five-days-per-week training results.

Practical Application

Although there are various exercise frequencies that produce excellent strength results, persons who train all of their muscles each workout may be best advised to follow a three-day-per-week training schedule. If this does not allow sufficient recovery and building time, consider training two days per week or using a split exercise routine. For example, you may choose to work your leg and midsection muscles on Mondays and Thursdays, and your torso and arm muscles on Tuesdays and Fridays.

Remember that more demanding exercise programs typically require more rest between training sessions. Finally, if you do not feel slightly stronger on successive workouts, you may need to change your training frequency.

Exercise Sets

There is a lack of consensus on how many sets you should perform for optimum strength development. Bodybuilders generally execute several exercise sets, whereas many individuals achieve excellent strength gains with single-set training.

DeLorme-Watkins Program

Following World War II, two medical doctors, Thomas DeLorme and Arthur Watkins (1948), experimented with strength training for purposes of muscle rehabilitation. Their work produced the first systematic and progressive weight-training program to receive approval from both medical and physical education professionals.

The DeLorme-Watkins program is based on the heaviest resistance that you can lift 10 times, called your 10 repetition maximum (10-RM) weightload. Set one consists of 10 repetitions with 50 percent of your 10-RM weightload. Set two consists of 10 repetitions with 75 percent of your 10-RM weightload. Set three consists of 10 repetitions with your 10-RM weightload.

Although the DeLorme-Watkins program involves three exercise sets, the first and second set serve as progressive warm-ups. The third set stresses the target muscles and provides the strength-building stimulus.

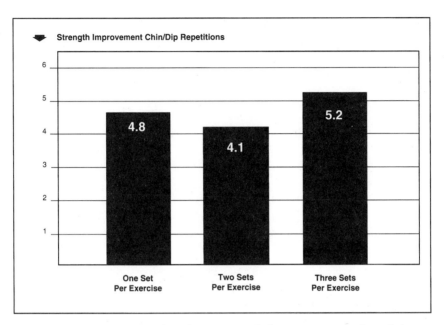

Figure 6.2 Comparison of one-, two-, and three-set strength training (77 subjects)

Berger Program

During the 1960s, Richard Berger conducted several studies to determine the optimum number of exercise sets and repetitions. His best known study (1962a) compared all combinations of one, two, and three sets with two, six, and ten repetitions per set. The results indicated that three sets of six repetitions each was most effective for promoting strength gains. Although subsequent research by Berger (1963) and O'Shea (1966) did not confirm the superiority of this program, three sets of six repetitions is a productive training protocol.

Single versus Multiple Sets

Westcott, Greenberger, and Milius (1989) examined all combinations of one, two, and three sets with 5, 10, and 15 repetitions per set. As presented in figure 6.2, all 77 subjects improved their chin-up and bar-dip performance over the 10-week training period.

However, statistical analyses showed no significant differences among the groups training with one, two, or three sets of exercise, nor among the groups training with 5, 10, or 15 repetitions per set.

Practical Application

Based on the results of these studies, the number of exercise sets you perform may be a matter of personal preference. However, it appears that the essential stimulus for strength development is one hard set of exercise.

If your first priority is training effectiveness, you may want to experiment with one, two, and three sets of strength exercise. If your first priority is exercise efficiency, you should attain excellent results with single-set strength training.

Recovery Intervals

If you choose a multiple-set training program, it is necessary to establish appropriate recovery intervals between successive work bouts for the same muscle group. Bodybuilders take very brief recovery intervals between sets because they are more concerned with pumping up their muscles than using heavy weightloads. Short recovery intervals accomplish this objective by maintaining blood congestion within the target muscles.

Weight lifters take relatively long recovery intervals between sets because they are more concerned with using heavy weightloads than pumping up their muscles. Long recovery intervals accomplish this objective by permitting full replenishment of muscle energy stores.

For purposes of basic strength building, recovery intervals of about two minutes are recommended. This is the time required to replenish over 90 percent of the muscle energy stores (see appendix D).

Practical Application

If you perform multiple-exercise sets, it may be advisable to establish consistent recovery intervals between repeated exercise bouts for the same muscle groups. If your primary objective is body-building, it may be preferable to take less than a one-minute recovery between successive exercise sets. If your primary objective is weight lifting, it may be advisable to take more than three minutes of recovery between successive exercise sets. If your primary objective is strength fitness, it is recommended to take about two minutes of recovery between successive exercise sets.

Exercise Resistance

Generally speaking, the exercise resistance for strength-building purposes should be relatively high. As noted in the Training Specificity section (chapter 3), strength is best developed by working within the anaerobic energy system. For most of us, the anaerobic energy system is best stressed by performing about 50 to 70 seconds of high-effort exercise.

It is therefore advisable to use a resistance that causes your target muscles to fatigue within 50 to 70 seconds. When exercising at a moderate movement speed (about 6 seconds per repetition), this is between 8 and 12 controlled repetitions.

As discussed in the next section, most individuals can complete 8 to 12 controlled repetitions with approximately 75 percent of their maximum resistance. That is, if you can perform one repetition with 100 pounds, you can most likely perform between 8 and 12 repetitions with 75 pounds. Seventy-five percent of maximum resistance is light enough to pose a low injury risk, and heavy enough to provide a high strength stimulus.

Practical Application

Seventy-five percent of maximum resistance is safe and effective for developing muscle strength. The most precise way to determine 75 percent of your maximum resistance is to first establish your maximum (1-RM) weightload. However, working with your maximum weightload may pose an unacceptable risk of injury. It is therefore recommended that you simply find a resistance that you can perform between 8 and 12 controlled repetitions. In most cases, this will correspond to approximately 75 percent of your maximum resistance.

Exercise Repetitions

There is an inverse relationship between resistance and repetitions. As the resistance increases the number of repetitions decreases, and vice-versa. Training with more than 90 percent of maximum resistance (4 or fewer repetitions) may have a high injury potential, and training with less than 60 percent of maximum resistance (16 or more repetitions) may have a low strength stimulus.

As presented in the Exercise Sets section, Berger (1962a) reported that 6 repetitions was more effective than 2 or 10 repetitions for building strength. However, in another study, Berger (1962b) found 3 to 9 repetitions equally effective for strength improvement. Later studies by Berger (1963), O'Shea (1966), and Withers (1970) all reported no significant differences when training with a variety of repetition protocols.

Jones (1986) conducted a considerable amount of research in the area of muscle endurance. He found that individuals with predominantly low-endurance muscle fibers (Type II) required few (5 to 6) repetitions to reduce their starting strength by 25 percent. Conversely, he found that individuals with predominantly high-endurance muscle fibers (Type I) required many (15 to 16) repetitions to reduce their starting strength by 25 percent. Jones suggested that differences in muscle endurance are due to inherent physiological characteristics that are not altered by training. If Jones's conclusion is correct, it may partly account for the inconsistent findings with regards to optimum exercise repetitions.

Repetitions with 75 Percent Maximum Resistance

Westcott (1986b, 1993g) examined differences in muscle performance with the same relative resistance (i.e., a given percentage of maximum resistance). One hundred forty-one males and females were tested for their maximum (1-RM) weightload on a Nautilus 10° chest machine. After a five-minute rest, the subjects performed as

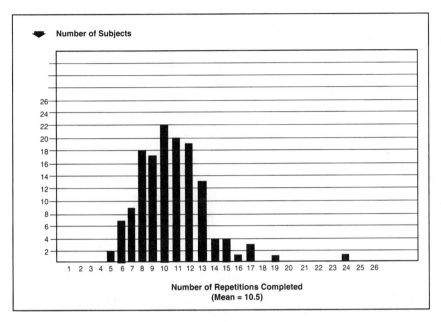

Figure 6.3 Distribution of repetitions completed with 75 percent of maximum weightload (141 subjects)

many repetitions as possible with 75 percent of their maximum weightload.

As shown in figure 6.3, most of the subjects completed 8 to 13 repetitions with 75 percent of their maximum resistance (mean = 10.5 repetitions). At six seconds per repetition, this represented approximately 50 to 70 seconds of high-effort exercise. The subjects who performed fewer than 8 repetitions were excellent power athletes (sprinters) who presumably have a higher percentage of fast-twitch (low-endurance) muscle fibers. The subjects who performed more than 13 repetitions were outstanding stamina athletes (distance runners) who presumably have a higher percentage of slow-twitch (high-endurance) muscle fibers.

Because all of the subjects had trained regularly in the same manner (one set of 8 to 12 repetitions), these findings seem to support Jones's (1986) contention that performance differences with the same relative resistance are due to inherent physiological characteristics. It is possible that our muscle fiber make-up may largely

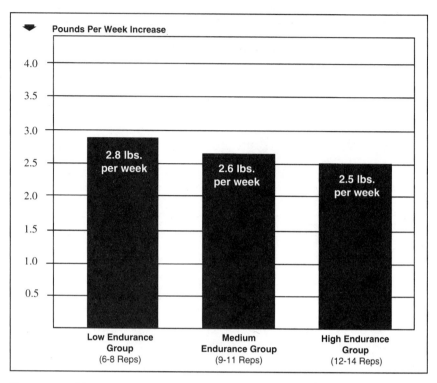

Figure 6.4 Changes in muscle strength for athletes training with low, medium, and high repetitions (13 subjects)

determine the number of repetitions we can perform with a given percentage of our maximum resistance.

Westcott (1987) conducted a two-month follow-up study with the track athletes who participated in the first repetitions study. Those who showed low-muscle endurance (less than 8 reps) trained with 6 to 8 repetitions. Those who showed medium muscle endurance (8 to 12 reps) trained with 9 to 11 repetitions. Those who showed high muscle endurance (more than 12 reps) trained with 12 to 14 repetitions.

All of the subjects increased their strength at the rate of almost 3 pounds per week (see figure 6.4). These results indicated that low-endurance muscles respond well to lower repetition training, medium-endurance muscles respond well to medium repetition training, and high-endurance muscles respond well to higher repetition training.

Practical Application

When using 75 percent of maximum resistance, most individuals can complete 8 to 13 controlled repetitions. Seventy-five percent of maximum is a safe and effective training resistance. Eight to 12 controlled repetitions require about 50 to 70 seconds of high-effort exercise, which provides an excellent strength stimulus. It is therefore recommended that most people train with about 8 to 12 repetitions per exercise set.

Persons with predominantly fast-twitch (low-endurance) muscle fibers may attain better results by training with fewer (4 to 8) repetitions per set. Persons with predominantly slow-twitch (high-endurance) muscle fibers may attain better results by training with more (12 to 16) repetitions per set. A method for estimating your muscle fiber type is presented in appendix C.

Exercise Progression

The key to strength development is progressive resistance exercise. In order to build stronger muscles you must gradually add more resistance to your training exercise. When you work your muscles a little harder than usual, they respond positively and become stronger. However, when you work your muscles a lot harder than usual, they respond negatively and become weaker or injured.

It is therefore important to plan your exercise progression in a systematic manner. Consider a double-progressive training system, in which you alternately increase the repetitions and the resistance. Let's say that you can perform 8 curls with 50 pounds. Train with 50 pounds until you can complete 12 curls, then increase the resistance to 52.5 pounds. The additional resistance may limit you to 10 repetitions. Train with 52.5 pounds until you can complete 12 curls, then increase the resistance to 55 pounds. Continue training in this double progressive manner to experience gradual strength gains with minimum injury risk.

As illustrated in figure 6.5, exercisers who take a gradual approach to strength development typically achieve better results because they have fewer overtraining setbacks.

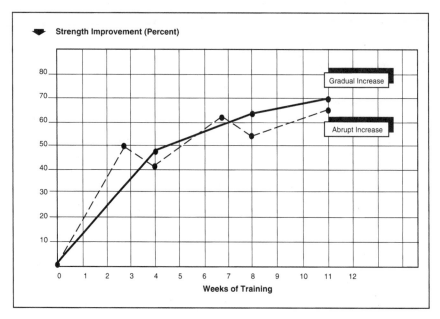

Figure 6.5 Typical progress curves for individuals who increase training stress gradually and individuals who increase training stress abruptly

Practical Application

Although there are many ways to increase your exercise resistance, it is important to do so in a systematic manner. One sensible approach is a double progressive program in which you increase the resistance by a small amount whenever you can complete 12 repetitions. As a rule, the exercise resistance should not be increased by more than 5 percent between successive training sessions. A strength-training logbook is recommended for monitoring progress and indicating gradual increments in resistance (see appendix E).

Exercise Periodization

When we make successive training sessions a little more demanding we will experience continuous strength development up to a point. Unfortunately, our bodies do not respond in this manner indefinitely. After several months of strength exercise, our muscles may require periodic variations in training stress to stimulate further adaptations.

Table 6–2 Sample three-month periodization program

Month	Exercise resistance	Exercise repetitions
First	About 65 percent maximum	12–16 reps per set
Second	About 75 percent maximum	8–12 reps per set
Third	About 85 percent maximum	4–8 reps per set

Exercise periodization is simply a systematic means for changing the training stimuli. Consider a sample three-month program of exercise periodization that progresses from higher repetitions with lower resistance to lower repetitions with higher resistance. As presented in table 6–2, the first-month training protocol is 12 to 16 repetitions with about 65 percent of maximum resistance. The lower resistance provides less stress to the muscles, tendons, ligaments, and bones, thereby reducing the risk of tissue injury during the initial conditioning phase.

The second-month training protocol is 8 to 12 repetitions with about 75 percent of maximum resistance. This is a basic strength-building period that provides a solid foundation for the final training phase.

The third-month training protocol is 4 to 8 repetitions with about 85 percent of maximum resistance. The higher resistance may provide greater strength stimulus, and should be well-tolerated by the muscles, tendons, ligaments, and bones after two months of progressive conditioning.

Following three months of regular resistance exercise, it may be advisable to take a week of active rest before repeating the training cycle. Active rest refers to non-strength-building activities such as walking, jogging, cycling, swimming, tennis, and basketball.

Although there are numerous periodization variations, the three-month training model fits well with most sports seasons. Repeating the training cycle provides a systematic change in the exercise stimulus. Assuming positive muscle adaptations, you should begin each new training cycle at a higher strength level.

Practical Application

Some form of exercise periodization may be advisable for long-term strength development. A basic three-month periodization program works well for most practical purposes. A general guideline

Table 6–3   Changes in muscle strength for subjects training with moderate and slow exercise speeds (74 subjects)

| Training group | (13 Exercises Total) | | |
	Beginning workload	Ending workload	Workload difference
Regular speed (n = 39)	588.0 lbs.	815.5 lbs.	+227.5 lbs.
Slow speed (n = 35)	581.5 lbs.	926.0 lbs.	+344.5 lbs.

is 12 to 16 repetitions with about 65 percent of maximum resistance during month one; 8 to 12 repetitions with about 75 percent of maximum resistance during month two; and 4 to 8 repetitions with about 85 percent of maximum resistance during month three. A week of active rest is recommended between the three-month training cycles.

Movement Speed

Since the 1970s there has been considerable debate regarding movement speed in strength exercise. Advocates of fast movement speed believe that it enhances explosive power (Counsilman 1976), whereas proponents of slow movement speed contend that it favors strength development and reduces injury potential (Pipes 1979).

Some studies (Moffroid and Whipple 1970; Coyle et al. 1981) revealed a specificity of training effect. That is, slower training appeared to be more effective when tested at slower speeds, and faster training appeared to be more effective when tested at faster speeds.

Other research (Westcott 1986a; Palmieri 1987) indicated that slower training produced strength gains when tested at slower speeds and faster speeds. Gettman and Ayres (1978) found that subjects who trained with slower movement speeds improved their body composition more than subjects who trained with faster movement speeds.

A study by Westcott (1994b) compared strength development for 198 subjects who trained with moderate to slow exercise speeds. As shown in Table 6–3, group A performed 4-second repetitions, group B performed 6-second repetitions, group C performed 8-second repetitions, and group D performed 14-second repetitions

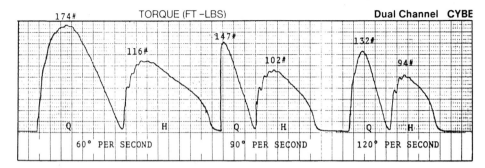

Figure 6.6 Isokinetic assessment of muscle force production at various movement speeds

(10 seconds lifting and 4 seconds lowering). All four groups made similar and significant strength gains over the eight-week training period. It would therefore appear that repetitions performed in 4, 6, 8 and 14 seconds are equally effective for increasing muscle strength when the exercise set is completed within the anaerobic energy system (30–90 seconds). However, a possible trend in favor of the very slow movement speed may indicate a need for further research.

Figure 6.6 shows a maximum effort knee extension (Q) and a maximum effort knee flexion (H) at three different movement speeds. You will note that as the movement speed increases, both the muscle tension (area of each force curve) and the muscle force (peak of each force curve) decrease. Research by Rosentswieg, Hinson, and Ridgway (1975) found significantly greater strength stimulus with slower muscle contractions. Van Oteghen (1975) also reported significantly greater strength development with slower speed training.

Although the research on movement speed is not conclusive, consider four advantages of training in a controlled manner.

1. *More muscle tension:* As shown in figure 6.6, slower movement speeds produce a longer period of muscle tension than faster movement speeds.

2. *More muscle force:* As shown in figure 6.6, slower movement speeds produce a higher level of muscle force than faster movement speeds.

3. *Less tissue trauma:* Although speed is essential in many athletic events, most are performed with body weight (e.g., high jump) or with a light implement (e.g., tennis racquet). Moving heavy

weights at fast speeds places great stress on your muscles and connective tissue. Slow strength training offers less tissue trauma and
lower injury risk.

4. *Less momentum:* The faster the lifting movement, the greater
the momentum. As the momentum component increases, the muscle component decreases. For example, bouncing the barbell off
your chest during the bench press exercise decreases the strength
stimulus and increases the injury potential.

Practical Application

Slower movement speeds are characterized by more muscle
tension, more muscle force, less tissue trauma, and less momentum.
For these reasons, you should perform strength exercise in a controlled manner. That is, you should be able to stop the resistance at
any point in the lifting or lowering movements. If you cannot do so,
you are probably training too fast.

Contraction Emphasis

Although we have one level of muscle force input, we have
three levels of force output. In a static (no movement) contraction,
our muscle force input and force output are essentially the same.
When a muscle shortens (positive contraction), internal friction decreases the force output by about 20 percent. When a muscle
lengthens (negative contraction), internal friction increases the force
output by about 20 percent.

Due to the differences in force output, many studies have been
conducted on contraction emphasis (Peterson 1960; Johnson 1972;
Atha 1981). Most have examined strength development resulting
from positive-only exercise, negative-only exercise, and positive-
negative exercise. The findings indicate similar strength gains for all
three training protocols.

Westcott (1992) compared positive-emphasis strength training
(lifting four seconds, lowering two seconds) and negative-emphasis
strength training (lifting two seconds, lowering four seconds) for 78
subjects. As shown in table 6–4, both the positive-emphasis group
and the negative-emphasis group made similar increases in muscle
strength and muscle mass over the eight-week training period.

Table 6–4 Changes in muscle strength and muscle mass for positive-emphasis and negative-emphasis training groups (78 subjects)

Exercise protocol	Mean change in muscle strength for 11 exercises	Mean changes in muscle mass
Positive emphasis (n = 51)	+24 lbs.	+2.9 lbs.
Negative emphasis (n = 27)	+25 lbs.	+3.1 lbs.

Practical Application

The key to strength development is resistance exercise that fatigues the target muscles within the anaerobic energy system. Apparently, positive-emphasis exercise and negative-emphasis exercise are equally effective for developing muscle strength and size. It is therefore suggested that contraction emphasis be a matter of personal preference, as long as you perform the lifting and lowering movements in a controlled manner.

Movement Range

A muscle becomes functionally stronger only in the movement range where it encounters progressive resistance exercise. It is therefore important to perform each exercise through a full range of movement. This strengthens the muscle at all joint positions and maintains joint flexibility.

It may be particularly useful to emphasize the fully contracted position of each exercise movement. When the target muscle group is fully contracted, the opposing muscle group is fully stretched.

Movement range should be a consideration when selecting your strength exercises. For example, chin-ups performed with a narrow grip provide more movement range and muscular work than chin-ups performed with a wide grip.

Practical Application

Strength exercises should be performed in a controlled manner through a complete range of joint movement. Do not force your muscles beyond their limits, but attempt to attain a reasonably stretched position and a fully contracted position with each repetition.

Training Time

Some people seem to function best in the morning, while others tend to be more energetic in the evening. Because most sports programs are held after school, athletes grow accustomed to training in the afternoon. While there are no definitive studies on training time, it is logical to assume that best results may be attained by training at a regular workout time.

It is also possible that general fatigue may influence our physical performance later in the day. As presented in chapter 2, our neck strength may decrease over 40 percent during the course of the day (see figure 2.1).

Practical Application

For best results, we should take our strength workouts when both our strength level and energy level are high. Although we may experience less general fatigue earlier in the day, training time is largely a matter of personal preference and practical availability.

Activity Order

Persons who perform strength exercise and endurance exercise during the same workout may be concerned with the order of activity. Westcott researched the effects of activity order on strength performance.

The first study (1986c) examined strength performance with and without prior endurance exercise. One session, the subjects performed 11 Nautilus exercises fresh, and the other session they performed 11 Nautilus exercises after 20 minutes of stationary cycling

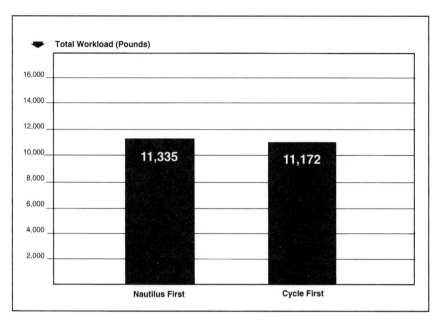

Figure 6.7 Effect of activity order on strength performance during 11-station Nautilus workout (8 subjects)

Table 6–5 Changes in muscle strength for subjects who did strength training first and subjects who did endurance training first (43 subjects)

Training protocol	Mean change in muscle strength for 11 exercises
Strength exercise first (n = 21)	+22 lbs.
Endurance exercise first (n = 22)	+23 lbs.

at 80 percent maximum heart rate. As shown in figure 6.7, their strength performance was essentially the same (1 percent difference) both sessions.

The second study (1993f) examined strength development over an eight-week training period. Forty-three men and women performed 11 Nautilus exercises and 20 minutes of endurance exercise during each workout. Half did the strength exercise first and half did the endurance exercise first. As shown in table 6–5, the strength gains were almost identical for both training groups.

Practical Application

Research indicates that strength training is equally effective when performed before or after moderate endurance activity, such as stationary cycling. Although endurance exercise may serve as an excellent warm-up for strength exercise, the best activity order is largely a matter of personal preference.

Exercise Breathing

It is important to breathe continuously during each exercise repetition. Holding your breath is a dangerous practice for two reasons. First, the internal pressure created by breath holding coupled with the external pressure of tightly contracted muscles may limit blood flow to the head and cause light-headedness. Second, the increased pressure in the chest area may limit blood return to the heart and cause significantly elevated blood pressure. This undesirable reaction is known as the Valsalva response and should be avoided.

From a physiological perspective, the best breathing pattern is to inhale during lowering movements (negative muscle contractions) and to exhale during lifting movements (positive muscle contractions). In this manner, the air pressure decreases as the muscular pressure increases, and vice-versa.

Practical Application

It is advisable to inhale during lowering movements and exhale during lifting movements. However, as long as you breathe regularly and do not hold your breath, you should not encounter problems.

Exercise Intensity

According to the American College of Sports Medicine (1990) statement on strength training, any amount of overload results in some strength development, but higher intensity effort produces a greater effect. Their guidelines recommend training to near muscle fatigue with each exercise set. Near muscle fatigue generally means working to a point where you can no longer lift the resistance.

Training to near muscle fatigue (sometimes called temporary muscle failure) is usually sufficient to stimulate strength development. However, upon reaching a strength plateau, it may be necessary to increase your training intensity for further strength gains. Five high-intensity strength-training techniques are presented in chapter 9.

Practical Application

For optimum strength development it is essential to fatigue the target muscle group within the anaerobic energy system. That is, use enough resistance to cause temporary muscle failure within approximately 50 to 70 seconds. For most practical purposes this represents about 8 to 12 repetitions performed with controlled speed, full range, and correct form.

Seven

Strength-training Effects

The long-term result of a sensible strength-training program is a well-developed musculoskeletal system that is both strong and injury-resistant. As discussed in chapter 2, progressive resistance exercise stimulates protein synthesis leading to larger muscles, and stronger tendons, ligaments, and bones.

Although these long-term effects are generally acknowledged and accepted, there is considerable confusion regarding the short-term effects of strength training. This chapter examines how strength exercise changes muscular strength, body composition, blood pressure, heart rate, and cardiovascular endurance.

Muscular Strength

Most people who begin a strength-fitness program are encouraged by relatively large strength gains during their first few weeks of training. However, the rate of strength development slows significantly as the training program continues, which may undermine exercise motivation unless the response factors are understood. For example, Westcott (1985a) observed strength improvements in six untrained women during eight weeks of supervised resistance exercise. The subjects were assessed for muscle strength (10-RM) at the beginning, midpoint, and end of the training program. As illustrated in figure 7.1, the women increased their overall muscle strength 76 percent during the first month, but only 13 percent during the second month. Although the participants improved their

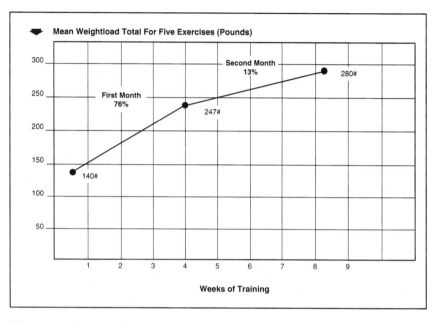

Figure 7.1 Percentage improvement during first and second months of strength training (6 subjects)

overall muscle strength 100 percent after eight weeks of training, three-quarters of the strength gain occurred during the first month.

A follow-up to that research (also Westcott 1985a) indicated that much of the initial strength development is specific to the exercises performed, and may be due to motor learning factors. After four weeks of strength training, the subjects made about 70 percent improvement on their leg exercises (10-RM Nautilus leg extension and 10-RM Nautilus leg curl). However, during the same period they recorded less than 10 percent improvement on independent isokinetic strength assessments (1-RM Cybex II leg extension and 1-RM Cybex II leg curl).

Research by Fukunaga (1976) showed a 60 percent strength increase during the first three weeks of training, but only a 30 percent strength increase over the next six weeks. His results revealed no increase in muscle mass during the first three weeks of training, but almost 10 percent increase in muscle mass over the next six weeks.

The findings of these studies indicate that early strength gains may be more closely related to neurological factors (improved muscle fiber recruitment), whereas later strength gains may be more closely related to physiological factors (increased muscle fiber size).

Summary

Many researchers believe that strength development is due first to improved muscle fiber recruitment, and second to increased muscle fiber size (Ikai and Fukunaga 1970; Moritani and DeVries 1979; Hakkinen and Komi 1983; McDonagh and Davies 1984; Fleck and Kraemer 1987). It is therefore important to continue your strength exercises even though the rate of improvement decreases. Although smaller, the subsequent strength gains are largely the result of additional muscle tissue.

Body Composition

Many people do not understand the difference between body-weight and body composition. They consider all weight loss desirable and all weight gain undesirable. Consequently those who are overweight typically want nothing to do with strength training because it builds muscle.

The fact is, most overweight individuals have too much fat weight but too little lean weight. As presented in chapter 2, adults lose about one-half pound of muscle every year through lack of use. This leads to a 0.5 percent per year decrease in metabolism, which is an underlying cause of weight (fat) gain. That is, calories that were used previously for muscle maintenance are deposited instead into fat storage.

The most popular approach to weight loss is a low-calorie diet. Unfortunately, dieting without exercise results in muscle loss and reduced metabolic rate (Zuti and Golding 1976; Clark 1985; Lamb 1988).

A better approach to fat loss is regular endurance exercise. This burns extra calories and improves cardiovascular fitness. However, endurance exercise is not very effective for replacing muscle tissue or increasing resting metabolism.

Strength training may be a more productive means for losing fat because it increases calorie utilization during exercise and at rest.

Table 7–1   Changes in body weight, fat, muscle, and body
composition for participants who performed strength and
endurance exercise with dieting (313 subjects)

Exercise program	Body weight change	Fat weight change	Muscle weight change	Body composition change
Strength and endurance	−5.0 lbs.	−8.0 lbs.	+3.0 lbs.	11.0 lbs.

The additional muscle developed through strength exercise has
high energy requirements, and elevates resting metabolism (Lamb
1985; Johnson 1986).

Westcott and Wessner (1993b) studied 313 men and women
who combined low-fat nutrition with 20 minutes of endurance exercise (walking, cycling, or stepping) and 20 minutes of strength exercise (eleven Nautilus exercises). After eight weeks of training the
subjects lost eight pounds of fat and gained three pounds of muscle,
for a five-pound weight loss and an eleven-pound improvement in
body composition see table 7–1). Instead of hurting their weight loss
effort, the additional muscle gave them larger engines and higher
daily energy requirements (Wilmore 1993).

Summary

Dieting is an effective means for decreasing fat weight, but it
may also reduce muscle mass and metabolic rate. Endurance exercise is effective for decreasing fat weight and improving cardiovascular fitness. However, it does not increase muscle mass or resting
metabolism. Strength exercise is effective for decreasing fat weight
and improving muscular fitness. In addition, it increases muscle
mass and resting metabolism. Because strength training results in
higher calorie use during both exercise and rest, it is an excellent
means for enhancing body composition.

Blood Pressure

Although physiologists agree that isometric strength exercise
can raise blood pressure to dangerous levels, there is less information on blood pressure response to dynamic strength exercise.

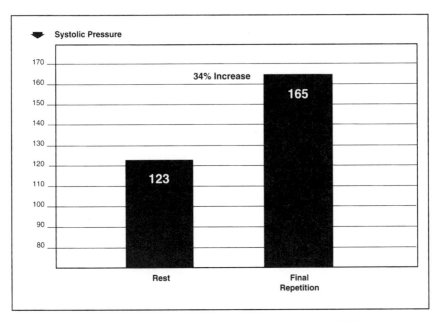

Figure 7.2 Systolic blood pressure response during 10-RM exercise set of one-arm dumbbell curls (24 subjects)

MacDougall et al. (1983) found an extremely high blood pressure response (400/300 mm Hg) in a bodybuilder during heavy leg training. It is possible that other factors (e.g., excessive body mass, essential hypertension, or anabolic steroids) may have been partly responsible for such a high reading (Wright 1978; Hunter and McCarthy 1982).

Freedson, Chang, and Katch (1984) reported blood pressures around 240/155 mm Hg for subjects performing free-weight and hydraulic bench press exercises. Westcott and Howes (1983) studied blood pressure response during one-arm dumbbell curls with the 10-RM weightload. As shown in figure 7.2, the 24 subjects' systolic blood pressure increased from 123 mm Hg at rest to 165 mm Hg during the final repetition. Their diastolic pressure measured 75 mm Hg before and immediately after the exercise set. Gender comparisons revealed higher systolic pressures for the male subjects, and age comparisons revealed higher systolic pressures for the older subjects (see table 7-2).

Table 7–2   Mean systolic blood pressure responses during ten-
repetition sets of one-arm dumbbell curls (24 subjects)

Subjects	Resting systolic pressure	Peak systolic pressure	Percent increase
All	123	165	34%
Males	131	179	37%
Females	114	148	29%
Over 38	132	175	33%
Under 38	115	154	34%

A follow-up study (Westcott 1986d) examined blood pressure response during Nautilus leg presses with the 10-RM weightload. As presented in figure 7.3, the 25 subjects' systolic blood pressure increased from 127 mm Hg at rest to 190 mm Hg during the final repetition. Their diastolic pressure measured 73 mm Hg before and 61 mm Hg immediately after the exercise set. Gender comparisons revealed higher systolic pressures for the male subjects, and age comparisons revealed higher systolic pressures for the older subjects (see table 7–3).

Another study (Westcott and Pappas 1987) assessed blood pressure response to circuit strength training. One hundred men and women performed one set of 11 Nautilus exercises with the 10-RM weightload. As presented in figure 7.4, the participants' pre-exercise blood pressure was 115/67 mm Hg and their one-minute postexercise blood pressure was 117/65 mm Hg.

A circuit strength-training study by Hurley et al. (1988) showed a significant reduction in diastolic blood pressure (84 to 79 mm Hg) following a sixteen-week program of resistance exercise. Harris and Holly (1987) also found a significant decrease in diastolic blood pressure (96 to 91 mm Hg) after a nine-week circuit strength-training program.

Westcott (1993b) recorded resting blood pressures for 263 adults before and after an eight-week fitness program (20 minutes of strength exercise and 20 minutes of endurance exercise). The participants experienced a six-mm Hg reduction in systolic blood pressure (134 to 128 mm Hg) and a three-mm Hg reduction in diastolic blood pressure (78 to 75 mm Hg).

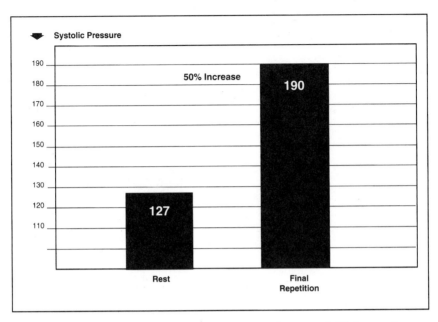

Figure 7.3 Systolic blood pressure response during 10-RM exercise set of Nautilus duo-squats (25 subjects)

Table 7–3 Mean systolic blood pressure responses during ten-repetition sets of Nautilus duo-squats (25 subjects)

Subjects	Resting systolic pressure	Peak systolic pressure	Percent increase
All	127	190	50%
Males	130	195	50%
Females	115	170	48%
Over 38	125	193	54%
Under 38	129	188	46%

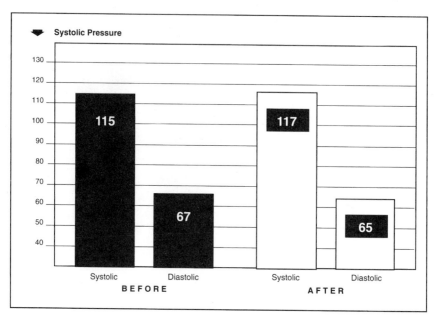

Figure 7.4 Blood pressure readings 30 to 60 seconds before and after performing an 11-station circuit strength training session (100 subjects)

Summary

Research with the 10-RM weightload shows systolic blood pressure increases of 35 percent (arm exercise) to 50 percent (leg exercise). Circuit strength-training studies reveal beneficial blood pressure adaptations when performed alone or in combination with endurance exercise.

Although sensible strength training should not cause adverse blood pressure responses, persons with elevated blood pressure or coronary risk factors should consult their physician before performing strength exercise. Sensible strength exercise is characterized by continuous movement and continuous breathing throughout every repetition. Isometric contractions and breath-holding should be avoided.

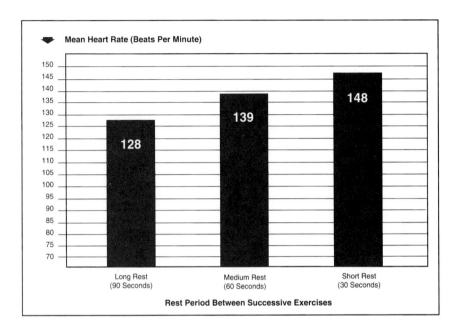

Figure 7.5 Mean peak heart rates for 10-station workout with long, medium, and short rests between successive exercises (30 subjects)

Heart Rate

Whenever the demand for energy increases, the heart rate increases. The heart is similar to the fuel pump in an automobile, and the muscles are analogous to the engine. As the muscles perform work, the heart must pump blood to the work site to replenish energy supplies and remove metabolic waste products. Because the heart pumps blood throughout the entire body, activity in any of the major muscle groups produces a faster heart rate. Although more oxygen is consumed by larger muscle groups, the heart-rate response is essentially the same for a leg extension and an arm extension (Hempel and Wells 1985).

Westcott (1985b) found a gradual and progressive increase in heart rate during ten repetitions with the 10-RM weightload. His findings also revealed higher mean heart rates when less time was taken between exercises. As illustrated in figure 7.5, when the 30 subjects took 90-second rests between exercises, their peak heart rates averaged 128 beats per minute. As the rest intervals decreased to 60 seconds and 30 seconds, their peak heart rates increased to 139 beats per minute and 148 beats per minute, respectively.

Summary

The heart-rate response and systolic blood-pressure response to dynamic strength training are similar in that both increase gradually, progressively, and predictably during an exercise set. The less rest taken between successive exercises, the higher the mean heart-rate response. The following case study illustrates a typical heart-rate and systolic blood-pressure response to a 10-exercise strength-training circuit.

Case Study: Heart Rate and Systolic Blood Pressure Responses to Strength Training

Subject: Mary Ellen   Age: 24   Workout Time: 19 Min.   Date: 3–31–86

		Heart Rate (BPM)	Systolic Blood Pressure (mm Hg)
Resting Values		78	120/78
Exercise	*Repetitions*		
Leg Extension	11	126	178
Leg Curl	12	138	212
Hip Adduction	12	112	200
Hip Abduction	12	143	222
Low Back	12	136	218
Abdominal	12	145	182
Pullover	10	114	178
Lateral Raise	10	112	192
Biceps Curl	10	110	182
Triceps Extension	12	105	202
Mean Exercise Values		124	197
30-Second Postexercise Values		99	124/70

Cardiovascular Function

Regular strength training may cause a reduction in resting blood-pressure readings (Stone, Wilson, and Blessing 1983; Hagberg et al. 1984; Harris and Holly 1987; Hurley et al. 1988). There is also evidence that strength training may improve lipoprotein and lipid profiles. Several studies have shown decreases in LDL (bad) cholesterol levels (Stone et al. 1982; Johnson et al. 1982; Goldberg et al. 1984; Hurley et al. 1988), and increases in HDL (good) cholesterol levels (Johnson et al. 1982; Goldberg et al. 1984; Hurley et al. 1988).

Other investigators have reported increased left ventricle wall thickness as a result of progressive strength training (Morganroth et al. 1975; Ricci, Lajoie, and Petitelerc 1982; Fleck et al. 1993). There are also indications that progressive strength training may increase muscle capillarization (Schantz 1982; McDonagh and Davies 1984). In addition, Peterson (1976); Stone, Wilson, and Blessing (1983); and Goldberg, Schutz, and Kloster (1983) found significant reductions in subjects' double products (heart rate X systolic blood pressure) after regular participation in a weight-training program.

These findings suggest that strength training may have some positive effects on the cardiovascular system. Other studies have attempted to determine whether strength training can increase aerobic capacity (maximum oxygen consumption). Improvements in aerobic capacity are typically observed when one regularly performs over 15 minutes of endurance exercise at an intensity sufficient to keep the heart rate above 75 percent of maximum (Zohman 1974; Ward 1988).

According to Hurley et al. (1984) and Hempel and Wells (1985), even though circuit strength training can maintain relatively high heart rates, it does not use a high enough percentage of maximum oxygen uptake to produce cardiovascular adaptations. However, Messier and Dill (1985) found a significant increase in maximum oxygen consumption after ten weeks of circuit strength training. In fact, the strength-program participants improved their maximum oxygen consumption as much as the subjects who participated in a running program. In a similar study, Harris and Holly (1987) found significant aerobic improvements in their subjects as a result of circuit strength training. One circuit strength-training program (Kelemen et al. 1986) showed significant cardiovascular improvement in cardiac rehabilitation participants, and another (Weltman et al. 1986) revealed significant aerobic increases in young boys.

Westcott and Warren (1985) conducted a circuit strength-training study with sedentary women, and found a 19 percent performance improvement on a standard cycle ergometer test. Because cycle exercise is related to both cardiovascular endurance and muscular strength, the subjects' 52 percent strength increase may have been largely responsible for their better posttraining results.

Summary

It is well-established that rhythmic endurance exercise such as jogging, cycling, and swimming are the preferred means for cardiovascular conditioning. However, there is evidence that strength exercise (especially circuit strength training) may provide several positive cardiovascular effects. These include reduced resting blood pressure, improved lipoprotein and lipid profiles, increased left ventricle wall thickness, increased muscle capillarization, reduced double products, and enhanced aerobic capacity.

Eight

Equipment and Safety Concerns

There are many approaches to strength training, and most produce some degree of muscle development. However, strength-training programs should also be evaluated in terms of injury potential. A well-designed strength-training program is as safe as it is effective.

Training Equipment

With respect to training equipment, the basic decision is whether to use free weights or machines. Free weights may be advantageous in terms of cost, convenience, and exercise variety. Barbell and dumbbell exercises also involve stabilizer muscles to provide necessary balance and control of the weights.

Machines may be advantageous in terms of exercise safety. For example, the dumbbell fly exercise and the 10° chest machine both target the pectoralis major and anterior deltoid muscles. However, the 10° chest machine provides a much better matching of muscle force and resistance force throughout the exercise movement.

In both exercises, your muscle force is lower in the bottom position (see figures 8.1a and 8.2a), and higher in the top position (see figures 8.1b and 8.2b). In the dumbbell fly, leverage makes the resistance force higher in the bottom position and lower in the top position. This provides a poor matching of muscle force and resistance force.

Figure 8.1a Dumbbell fly (bottom position)

In the 10° chest machine, a counter-leverage system (the cam) makes the resistance force lower in the bottom position and higher in the top position. This provides a good matching of muscle force and resistance force.

Unlike the dumbbell fly exercise, the 10° chest machine automatically varies the resistance force in accordance with your muscle force. This reduces the risk of injury, and may make the exercise more productive.

Training Space

Be aware of space limitations when performing strength exercise. Few things present a greater safety threat than too little training space, especially if you are exercising with other people. Whether you train at home or in a fitness center, make sure that

Figure 8.1b Dumbbell fly (top position)

there is ample space to perform each exercise without interference or restrictions.

Training Partners

Another important safety consideration is the use of spotters for certain barbell exercises such as squats, bench presses, and incline presses. In each of these exercises, failure to raise the barbell from the bottom position may lead to serious injury. It is therefore essential to train with a spotter when performing these exercises. The spotter should give you plenty of space to perform the exercise movement but be ready to help the moment assistance is required.

Figure 8.2a A 10° chest machine (bottom position)

In the squat, the spotter should stand behind you and move up and down in tandem. If your upward movement stalls out, the spotter should wrap his arms around your chest and help you to a standing position. In the bench press and incline press, the spotter may assist you in removing the barbell and then replacing it on the standards. If you need assistance to complete the pressing movement, the spotter should grasp the barbell firmly and help you lift it onto the standards.

Spotters are excellent sources of encouragement and essential for most high-intensity training sessions. Whenever possible, it is advisable to train with a competent and caring spotter.

Training Technique

Perhaps the most important safety consideration is training technique. Undoubtedly, improper exercise technique is responsible for more strength-training injuries than all other causes combined.

Figure 8.2b A 10° chest machine (top position)

Most strength-training injuries result from too much weight, too much speed, and too little support.

When too much weight is used for the target muscles to handle, additional muscle groups are utilized to produce momentum. Momentum-assisted weight lifting is a dangerous procedure because it subjects the muscles and connective tissue to high stress levels.

Too much speed has a similar effect on muscle and connective tissue. Fast exercise speeds require excessive force at the beginning of each lifting movement, thereby increasing the risk of injury.

Too little support is a frequent cause of low-back injuries. This is especially true when trying to lift too much weight overhead in

Figure 8.3 Unsupported overhead press

an unsupported barbell press. As illustrated in figures 8.3 and 8.4, unsupported pressing movements place considerably more stress on the low-back area than supported pressing movements.

Proper training technique is beneficial for increasing muscle strength and decreasing injury risk. Make it a priority to exercise with appropriate weight loads, controlled speeds, and supportive structures whenever possible.

Figure 8.4 Supported overhead press

Nine

Advanced Strength Training

After your body has adjusted to the basic strength-training program, advanced strength training will stimulate further muscle development.

Strength Plateaus

Periods of little or no performance improvement are called strength plateaus. Strength plateaus simply indicate that some aspect of your training protocol should be changed.

Although there may be other training considerations (equipment, sleep, diet, partners, etc.), the basic decision is whether to make your workout more demanding or less demanding. Most exercisers work harder in an attempt to force further strength development. In many cases, this strategy either maintains the strength plateau or results in strength loss. Doing more of the same exercise routine that led to the strength plateau seldom initiates new strength gains. A better approach is to examine your exercise program and make constructive changes in the training variables.

Change in Training Variables

One approach for overcoming a strength plateau is to change one or more of the training variables. These include exercise selection, exercise frequency, exercise sets, and repetition-resistance relationships.

Exercise Selection

The first step may be a change in your training exercises. For example, if progress comes to a halt in the bench press, substitute it with the incline press. While both exercises utilize the same muscle groups (chest, shoulders, and triceps), the different movement patterns elicit different muscular responses. Changing your training exercises can stimulate further improvement in both exercise performance and muscle development.

Exercise Frequency

The second consideration has to do with exercise frequency. It is sometimes helpful to reduce your workout demands temporarily to allow the muscle recovery and building process to catch up. Keep in mind that positive muscle adaptations occur during the rest periods following your training sessions. Consequently, it may be beneficial to schedule more time between successive workouts when facing a strength plateau.

Exercise Sets

A third alternative is to increase or decrease the number of sets per exercise. If you have difficulty training in a high-intensity manner, you may benefit from additional exercise sets. On the other hand, if you are making little progress with multiple-set training, you may achieve better results with a single-set exercise program. As a rule, the more exercises performed, the fewer sets per exercise.

Repetition-Resistance Relationship

Another area that should be examined is the repetition-resistance relationship. It may be helpful to complete more repetitions at a lower resistance or to perform fewer repetitions at a higher resistance. For example, your quadriceps muscles may be so accustomed to performing 12 repetitions with 140 pounds that this training protocol no longer promotes strength gains. In this case, switching to 8 repetitions with 160 pounds may stimulate additional strength development. Occasional variations in your repetitions-resistance relationship seem to be an effective means for reducing both physical and mental staleness.

Increase in Training Intensity

The basic philosophy of high-intensity strength training is to make your muscles work harder than usual while still reaching temporary failure within your anaerobic energy system (under 90 seconds). Many people confuse exercise duration with exercise intensity. Doing more sets of an exercise increases the training duration, but not necessarily the training intensity.

Let's say that you can perform one barbell curl with 100 pounds (maximum resistance), and ten barbell curls with 75 pounds (75 percent of maximum resistance). When you can no longer lift 75 percent of your maximum resistance, you have reduced your starting strength by 25 percent. Because each set of 75-pound barbell curls fatigues 25 percent of your biceps muscle fibers, performing more sets does not increase the training intensity.

One way to increase the training intensity is to fatigue more muscle fibers. This objective may be safely achieved by continuing the exercise set with a reduced resistance. For example, when you can no longer curl 75 pounds, drop the weight to 60 pounds and complete three or four additional repetitions. In this manner, you experience muscle failure twice during an extended exercise set, and you fatigue 40 percent of your biceps muscle fibers.

Westcott (1994) trained 60 previously sedentary men and women for two months. During the first month, all of the subjects performed one set of each exercise with a resistance that fatigued the target muscles within 8–12 repetitions. During the second month, 27 subjects followed the same training protocol, while 33 subjects continued each exercise set with a reduced resistance. That is, when they could no longer lift the initial resistance, they quickly decreased the weight about 20 percent and completed a few more repetitions. Over the course of the training period, the high-intensity exercise group increased their muscle strength significantly more than the standard exercise group.

Hypothetical Muscle Fiber Response Pattern

The neurological and physiological components of muscle force production are extremely complex. However, based on what is understood about these neuromuscular processes, consider the following hypothetical model of muscle fiber recruitment during a set of biceps curls with a 40-pound dumbbell.

First, let's assume that you have an even mix of Type I (slow-twitch) and Type II (fast-twitch) fibers in your biceps muscle. As shown in the simplified schematic diagram (see figure 9.1), you have seven Type I fibers and seven Type II fibers.

Second, let's assume that your fast-twitch fibers are composed of four Type IIA (fast-twitch, more endurance) and three Type IIB (fast-twitch, less endurance).

Third, let's assume that each Type I fiber produces 5 pounds of force, and fatigues between 12–16 contractions (repetitions). Let's assume that each Type IIA fiber produces 6 pounds of force, and fatigues after 2 contractions (repetitions). Let's assume that each Type IIB fiber produces 7 pounds of force and fatigues after 1 contraction (repetition).

When you curl the 40-pound dumbbell, you recruit the necessary number of muscle fibers beginning with the Type I fibers, followed by the Type IIA fibers, followed by the Type IIB fibers. As illustrated in figure 9.1, lifting a 40-pound resistance requires all seven Type I fibers and one Type IIA fiber (35 pounds of force plus 6 pounds of force = 41 pounds of force).

The activated Type IIA fiber functions for two repetitions, then fatigues and cannot contribute further to this exercise set. The second Type IIA fiber provides force for two more repetitions, as do the third and fourth Type IIA fibers.

After eight repetitions all of the Type IIA fibers are fatigued, and the first Type IIB fiber is activated for the ninth repetition. It provides force for one repetition, as do the second and third Type IIB fibers.

After 11 repetitions, there are too few functioning muscle fibers to lift 40 pounds, so you set the dumbbell down. Following a brief

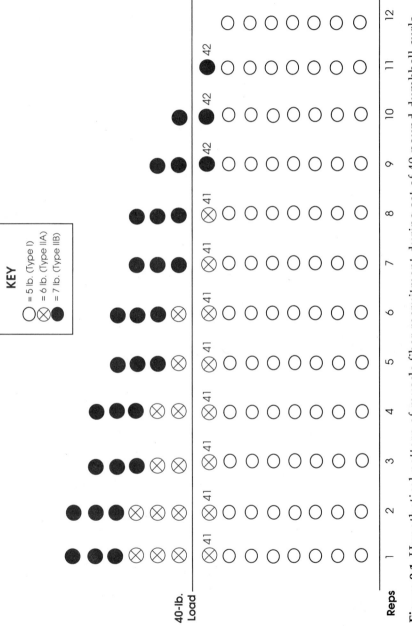

Figure 9.1 Hypothetical pattern of muscle fiber recruitment during set of 40 pound dumbbell curls

recovery period (about two minutes to replenish the phosphocreatine energy stores), you perform a second set of dumbbell curls. Because the fiber activation pattern is the same, you fatigue the same muscle fibers in the same recruitment order during each successive set of dumbbell curls.

While there is nothing wrong with training in this manner, the emphasis is on the duration of the exercise rather than the intensity of the exercise. The basic intent of high intensity strength training is to provide a different or a deeper stimulus to the muscle fibers.

For example, with breakdown and assisted training, you reduce the resistance at the point of failure so that you can perform a few more repetitions and fatigue a few more muscle fibers. With super-set training, you provide sequential but different exercise movements that activate different muscle fibers in a different recruitment pattern. Negative-only training increases muscle stress by means of more resistance, and slow training increases muscle tension by means of reduced momentum.

While traditional strength-training methods are certainly effective, high-intensity techniques provide efficient and productive exercise alternatives. Due to the greater muscle demands and longer tissue-building period, high-intensity training should be used prudently. With the exception of genetically gifted bodybuilders, one high-intensity exercise session per week should be sufficient for optimum muscle development. If working harder makes more sense than working longer, consider the following high-intensity strength-training techniques.

Breakdown Training

Breakdown training refers to reducing the exercise resistance at the point of muscle failure. Generally, a 20 percent weightload decrease will permit three or four additional repetitions. For best results, the transition from regular to reduced resistance should be as brief as possible. Breakdown training is an effective means for stimulating muscle development as long as it is not overdone. It is not recommended to reduce the weightload more than once per exercise. In fact, for best results, the extended exercise set should be completed within the range of the anaerobic energy system (about 90 seconds).

Assisted Training

Another high-intensity training technique, known as assisted training, accomplishes the same objective with the help of a partner. Instead of reducing the resistance at the point of muscle failure, a partner assists you with a few additional repetitions. To be most effective, your partner provides just enough assistance for you to complete the lifting (positive) movement, but allows you to perform the lowering (negative) movement on your own. Because your negative-force output is greater than your positive-force output, assisted training is productive during both the lifting and lowering movement of each additional repetition. Three or four assisted repetitions enable you to fatigue more muscle fibers during the extended set of high-effort exercise.

Super-Set Training

While there are variations of super-set training, the basic procedure requires two successive exercises for the target muscle group. Generally, the first exercise is a rotary movement, and the second exercise is a linear movement. For example, the chest cross (rotary) exercise is performed to exhaust the pectoralis major muscles (see figure 9.2a). At the point of muscle failure, the chest press (linear) exercise is performed to further stress the pectoralis major muscles (see figure 9.2b). This is possible because the different movement pattern activates different muscle fibers, and fresh triceps muscles assist the fatigued pectoralis major muscles in the chest press exercise. For best results, move immediately from the rotary exercise to the linear exercise.

Super-set training is an effective means for pushing a muscle group beyond its normal limits. However, it is not advisable to carry super-set training to extremes, as overtraining problems may result. One super-set per muscle group is a reasonable guideline for this advanced training technique.

Negative-Only Training

Negative-only training enables you to use heavier weightloads because you can lower about 40 percent more resistance than you can lift. While this provides greater training stress, it also increases

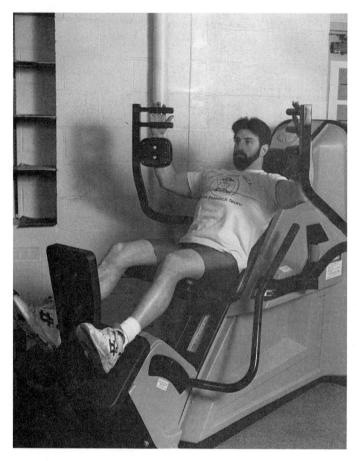

Figure 9.2a Chest cross (rotary) exercise involves pectoralis major muscles.

the risk of tissue injury. Therefore, negative-only training should always be performed in a controlled manner.

One form of negative-only training requires a partner to help lift a heavier weightload than you can lift yourself. You slowly lower the resistance through the full movement range. Due to the inherent risk in this training method, use just a little more weight than you can lift on your own.

Another type of negative-only training involves bodyweight exercises such as pull-ups and bar dips. If you are not strong enough to lift your bodyweight, simply climb to the top position and slowly

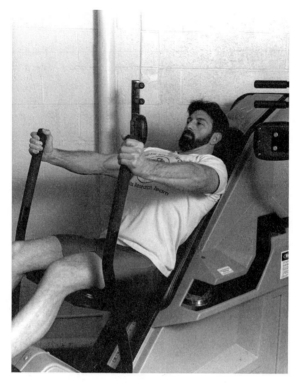

Figure 9.2b Chest press (linear) exercise involves pectoralis major and triceps muscles.

lower yourself to the bottom position. The same muscles used positively to lift your bodyweight are used negatively to lower your bodyweight.

Slow Training

Another means for making each training set more difficult is to slow the movement speed. Slower movements involve less momentum and require more muscle force throughout the entire joint range of motion.

One study (Westcott 1993f) compared the strength gains of two closely-matched exercise groups after two months of training. Both groups performed one set of exercise for each of the major muscle groups. The training procedures were identical except for the movement speeds. One group of 39 subjects performed 10 repetitions per set at seven seconds per rep (two seconds up, one second pause, four seconds down). The other group of 35 subjects performed 5 repetitions per set at 14 seconds per rep (ten seconds up and four seconds down). The data trend (see table 6–3) suggested that slower-speed strength training may be more effective for increasing muscle strength than faster-speed training.

Summary

When practiced properly, all five high-intensity training techniques produce greater muscle stress, and require longer recovery/ building periods. Therefore, you should not perform high-intensity training too frequently. Sufficient sleep and quality nutrition are also important considerations during periods of high-effort strength exercise.

Strength plateaus appear to be an inevitable consequence of continued training. Regardless of the exercise protocol you follow, there comes a time when change is necessary to stimulate further strength development. These program modifications should be viewed as positive steps toward achieving your full muscular potential.

Ten

Bodybuilding and Strength Building

Almost everyone who follows a sensible strength-training program experiences a significant degree of muscular development. That is, there is a definite improvement in muscle strength and physical appearance.

While strength exercise produces larger muscle fibers, it does not always produce larger arms or legs. In many cases, the muscle gain is matched by an equal fat loss. However, properly performed strength training does lead to firm, fit, functional muscles that may encourage you to pursue higher levels of development. If you are interested in more muscular size, you may experiment with specific bodybuilding programs. If you are interested in more muscular strength, you may explore specific strength-building programs.

Although basic bodybuilding and strength-building programs are related, there are differences in the actual training methods. Table 10–1 presents five key training variables associated with typical bodybuilding and strength-building programs, as well as guidelines for a combination program.

Exercises Per Muscle Group

Most bodybuilders perform several exercises for each major muscle group. Intermediate bodybuilders typically perform three to five exercises for the thighs, abdominals, chest, upper back,

Table 10–1   Five key training variables associated with typical bodybuilding and strength-building programs

Training variables	Bodybuilding program	Strength-building program	Combination program
1. Exercise per muscle group	3–5 exercises	1–2 exercises	2–3 exercises
2. Sets per exercise	3–5 sets	4–6 sets	3–4 sets
3. Repetitions per set	10–15 reps	1–5 reps	5–10 reps
4. Recovery time between sets	less than 1 minute	more than 3 minutes	about 2 minutes
5. Training days per week	6 days	3 days	4 days

shoulders, biceps, and triceps. In addition, they generally include one or two exercises for the neck, upper trapezius, lower back, oblique, calf, and forearm muscles.

The main reason bodybuilders perform so many exercises is to stimulate more muscle fibers. Because each strength exercise elicits a specific response, a variety of exercises involves more fibers and provides more stimulus for muscle growth.

On the other hand, strength builders are not as concerned about increasing their muscle size. Rather, they strive to achieve high levels of strength performance in specific exercises, such as the squat, deadlift, power clean, bench press, and overhead press. The squat, deadlift, and power clean exercises involve the large muscles of the thigh, buttocks, and lower back. The bench press and overhead press emphasize the muscles of the chest, shoulders, and triceps. Because careless performance of these exercises may place excessive stress on the low back, it is essential to use proper form throughout each movement.

Although most strength builders include additional exercises, they seldom perform more than two exercises per muscle group. This is largely due to time constraints, as strength builders typically complete several sets of each exercise with relatively long recovery periods between sets.

Sets Per Exercise

As a rule, both bodybuilders and strength builders perform several sets of each exercise. However, there are notable differences in their training objectives and procedures. The principal reasons bodybuilders do numerous sets are: (1) to stimulate the muscle fibers repetitively and (2) to pump up the muscle tissue.

Performing many sets of exercise with brief rests causes large quantities of blood to accumulate in the muscles, increasing their size temporarily. Although not well understood, this temporary muscle enlargement (muscle pump) contributes to the development of larger muscles.

Strength builders perform numerous sets of exercise for other reasons. First, in order to maximize strength, it is necessary to train with heavy resistance. Often strength builders work up to the heaviest weight load they can lift for a single repetition. In order to exercise safely and effectively with such high resistance, they must prepare their muscles for maximum effort by performing progressively heavier warm-up sets. Consequently, the strength builder who ends a workout with a maximum bench press of 300 pounds might perform preliminary sets as follows:

140 pounds × 8 repetitions
180 pounds × 6 repetitions
220 pounds × 4 repetitions
260 pounds × 2 repetitions
300 pounds × 1 repetition

Like bodybuilders, strength builders also perform several sets of exercise to stimulate the muscle fibers repetitively. However, because strength builders are more concerned with muscle performance than muscle pump, they typically rest much longer between sets. For example, a strength builder may perform four sets of leg extensions with 200 pounds and 3-minute rests, whereas a bodybuilder may perform four sets of leg extensions with 150 pounds and 30-second rests.

Repetitions Per Set

Some individuals have a majority of low-endurance muscle fibers (Type II) and should generally exercise with fewer repetitions per set. Others have a majority of high-endurance muscle fibers (Type I) and should typically train with more repetitions per set. However, there are additional factors that must be considered in bodybuilding and strength building.

For bodybuilders to achieve a satisfactory muscle pump, they must perform a reasonably high number of repetitions. Generally speaking, bodybuilders average 10 to 15 repetitions per set and occasionally complete as many as 20 repetitions per set.

On the other hand, strength builders exercise with very heavy resistance to facilitate strength gains, thereby necessitating a lower number of repetitions. Because maximum attempts are not uncommon, strength builders usually train with weight loads they can lift for 1 to 5 repetitions.

When coupled with short rest periods between sets, 10 to 15 repetitions is an effective training range for enhancing muscle size. When coupled with long rest periods between sets, 1 to 5 repetitions is a productive training range for increasing muscle strength.

Recovery Time between Sets

One of the most critical differences between bodybuilding and strength building is the recovery time between sets of exercise. As mentioned earlier, bodybuilders typically take short rests between sets to maintain blood accumulation within the muscle. This results in temporary muscle enlargement and is referred to as pumping up the muscles. Short-rest strength training is accompanied by considerable muscle discomfort due to blood congestion, lactic acid production, energy depletion, and tissue fatigue. Most bodybuilders rest no more than 30 to 60 seconds between exercise sets. While this is not the only means for building larger muscles, short rest intervals are characteristic of successful bodybuilding programs.

Strength builders place greater emphasis on muscle performance than muscle appearance, and therefore do not intentionally train for a muscle pump. Because exercise resistance is directly related to strength development, strength builders generally train with very heavy weight loads. Of course, this type of training requires relatively long recovery periods for successful performance. This is necessary to establish normal blood flow, remove lactic acid, replenish energy sources, and reduce tissue fatigue. Although the time frame varies among individuals, most strength builders average over three minutes of rest between exercise sets.

Training Days Per Week

Bodybuilders spend a lot of time in the exercise facility. Due to the intense nature of their training program, they generally do not work all of their major muscle groups during a single session. Some bodybuilders follow a two-part split routine, working their legs and lower body on a Monday-Wednesday-Friday sequence and their arms and upper body on a Tuesday-Thursday-Saturday sequence. Others subscribe to a three-part split routine, typically working their back and biceps on Mondays and Thursdays, their chest and triceps on Tuesdays and Fridays, and their legs and shoulders on Wednesdays and Saturdays. It is important to note, however, that they do not exercise the same muscle group two days in succession.

Conversely, the majority of strength builders take a complete day of rest and recovery between exercise sessions. At the very least, strength builders may perform all of their exercises on Monday, rest Tuesday, perform all of their exercises again on Wednesday, rest Thursday, etc. However, because heavy training typically requires longer recovery and building periods, an advanced strength builder may emphasize leg exercises on Monday, torso exercises on Wednesday, and a combination of exercises on Friday.

Although specific training schedules vary from individual to individual, it is safe to say that most bodybuilders average six exercise days per week, and that the majority of strength builders average three or four exercise days per week.

Sample Bodybuilding Program

If you possess the genetic potential and personal motivation to become a bodybuilder, you may consider a more comprehensive training program. Table 10–2 presents a sample bodybuilding protocol based on a three-part split routine.

Table 10–2 Sample training program for intermediate bodybuilders

Mondays and Thursdays (back, biceps, abdominals)

Back exercises

Deadlift	3 sets (12–10–8)	60 sec. rest
Pulldown	3 sets (12–10–8)	60 sec. rest
Seated row	3 sets (12–10–8)	60 sec. rest
Pullover machine	3 sets (12–10–8)	60 sec. rest
Chin-up	3 sets (10–8–6)	45 sec. rest

Biceps exercises

Standing curl	4 sets (12–10–8–6)	45 sec. rest
Incline dumbbell curl	4 sets (12–10–8–6)	45 sec. rest
Preacher curl	4 sets (12–10–8–6)	45 sec. rest
Biceps machine	4 sets (12–10–8–6)	30 sec. rest

Abdominal exercises

Abdominal machine	3 sets (12–10–8)	30 sec. rest
Trunk curl/weight	3 sets (20–15–10)	30 sec. rest
Rotary torso machine	2 sets (12/12–10/10)	30 sec. rest

Tuesdays and Fridays (chest, triceps, neck, forearms)

Chest exercises

Bench press	4 sets (12–10–8–6)	60 sec. rest
Incline press	3 sets (12–10–8)	60 sec. rest
Cross chest machine	3 sets (12–10–8)	60 sec. rest
10-degree chest machine	3 sets (12–10–8)	60 sec. rest
Bar-dip	3 sets (10–8–6)	45 sec. rest

Triceps exercises

Pressdown	4 sets (12–10–8–6)	45 sec. rest
Lying extension	4 sets (12–10–8–6)	45 sec. rest
Triceps machine	4 sets (12–10–8–6)	45 sec. rest
Standing extension	4 sets (12–10–8–6)	30 sec. rest

Neck exercises

Neck flexor machine	3 sets (12–10–8)	45 sec. rest
Neck extensor machine	3 sets (12–10–8)	45 sec. rest

Forearm exercises

Wrist roll	2 sets (8/8–6/6)	60 sec. rest

Wednesdays and Saturdays (legs, shoulders, calves)

Leg exercises		
Squat	4 sets (12–10–8–6)	60 sec. rest
Leg extension machine	4 sets (12–10–8–6)	60 sec. rest
Leg curl machine	4 sets (12–10–8–6)	60 sec. rest
Leg press machine	4 sets (12–10–8–6)	60 sec. rest
Hip adductor machine	3 sets (12–10–8)	60 sec. rest
Hip abductor machine	3 sets (12–10–8)	60 sec. rest
Shoulder exercises		
Standing press	4 sets (12–10–8–6)	60 sec. rest
Upright row	4 sets (12–10–8–6)	45 sec. rest
Lateral raise machine	4 sets (12–10–8–6)	45 sec. rest
Neck/shoulder machine	3 sets (12–10–8)	30 sec. rest
Calf exercises		
Standing heel raise	3 sets (12–10–8)	30 sec. rest
Seated heel raise	3 sets (12–10–8)	30 sec. rest

Sample Strength-building Program

If you have the physical ability and personal desire to become a strength builder, you may consider a more specialized training program. Table 10–3 presents a sample strength-building protocol based on a three-day training schedule.

Both bodybuilding and strength-building programs require a lot of time and effort. Examine your personal objectives, your physical potential, and your training commitment. If everything is in order, review the sample programs, experiment with the exercise variables, and take a progressive approach toward performance improvement.

Table 10–3 Sample training program for intermediate strength
builders

Monday		
Barbell squat	6 sets progressive (8–6–4–2–2–2)	3 min. rest
Leg extension	4 sets (6–6–6–6)	3 min. rest
Leg curl	4 sets (6–6–6–6)	3 min. rest
Pulldown	4 sets (6–6–6–6)	3 min. rest
Seated row	4 sets (6–6–6–6)	3 min. rest
Standing curl	4 sets (6–6–6–6)	3 min. rest
Heel raise	4 sets (8–8–8–8)	2 min. rest
Wednesday		
Bench press	6 sets progressive (8–6–4–2–2–2)	3 min. rest
Standing press	4 sets (6–6–6–6)	3 min. rest
Bar-dip	4 sets (6–6–6–6)	3 min. rest
Pressdown	4 sets (6–6–6–6)	3 min. rest
Lateral raise machine	4 sets (8–8–8–8)	3 min. rest
Shrug	4 sets (4–4–4–4)	2 min. rest
Friday		
Deadlift	6 sets progressive (8–6–4–2–2–2)	3 min. rest
Power clean	6 sets progressive (8–6–4–2–2–2)	3 min. rest
Abdominal machine	4 sets (8–8–8–8)	3 min. rest
Low-back machine	4 sets (6–6–6–6)	3 min. rest
Rotary torso machine	2 sets (6/6–6/6)	3 min. rest
Wrist roll	2 sets (6/6–6/6)	2 min. rest
Tuesday, Thursday, Saturday and Sunday are recovery days		

Eleven

Strength Training for Youth and Seniors

Whether eight or eighty, our bodies respond in a similar manner to progressive-resistance exercise. Regular strength-training stimuli produce musculoskeletal responses regardless of age factors. In fact, research indicates that youth strength trainers gain muscle size and strength more rapidly than adult strength trainers due to normal growth and maturation processes (Westcott 1991a; Faigenbaum et al. 1992).

At the other end of the age continuum, seniors seem to experience similar rates of muscle and strength development as younger adults (Evans and Rosenberg 1991; Munnings 1993; Westcott 1993a). This may be due to more atrophied muscles that tend to respond quickly to appropriate strength stimuli.

Youth and seniors are similar in another aspect. During the youth years of tissue development and the senior years of tissue degeneration, our bodies are more susceptible to injuries. It is therefore important to provide competent instruction and careful supervision to persons in the "body change" age ranges.

Research Findings—Youth

For many years it was assumed that strength training posed an unacceptable risk of injury to children, particularly with respect to bone growth-plate damage. However, there are no reports of bone

---

Table 11–1 Changes in body composition and muscle strength for teenagers who did and teenagers who did not perform resistance exercise (19 subjects)

	Strength trainers (n = 14)	Control subjects (n = 5)
Bodyweight	+3 lbs.	+3 lbs.
Percent fat	−1%	+0.5%
Lean weight	+4 lbs.	+2 lbs.
Fat weight	−1 lb.	+1 lb.
Leg extension strength (10 RM)	+63%	+8%

growth-plate injuries to preadolescent participants in supervised strength-training programs (National Strength and Conditioning Association 1985).

Likewise, it has long been contended that preadolescents are incapable of exercise-induced strength gains due to low hormone (testosterone) levels. However, studies by Servedio et al. (1985), Sewall and Micheli (1986), Weltman et al. (1986), and Faigenbaum et al. (1992) have demonstrated significant strength increases in preteen boys and girls who performed resistance exercise.

Faigenbaum et al. (1992) examined strength improvements in prepubescent children (average age 10 years) who strength trained twice a week for eight weeks. The program participants increased their overall muscle strength by 74 percent, while the control subjects increased their overall muscle strength by 13 percent.

Westcott (1993c) reported body composition and strength changes in 67 boys and girls (average age 11 years) who followed a basic resistance-training program (three days per week, six exercises, one set of 8 to 12 repetitions). After two months of training the subjects added 4.0 pounds of lean weight, lost 2.5 pounds of fat weight, and increased their muscle strength by 58 percent.

Research with teenagers has produced similar findings. In one study (Westcott 1991a), 14 boys and girls (average age 14 years) completed a basic resistance-training program (three days per week, eight exercises, one set of 8 to 12 repetitions). After two months of training the teenagers added 4.0 pounds of lean weight, lost 1.0 pound of fat weight, and increased their muscle strength by 63 percent. As shown in table 11–1, the control subjects (average age 14 years) also added lean weight due to normal maturation. However, there was a significant difference in strength development between the training and nontraining groups.

Research findings clearly indicate that sensible strength training is a safe and effective physical activity for preteen and teenage boys and girls. However, it is imperative that youth strength-training programs be conducted in a carefully structured and closely supervised exercise environment.

Training Recommendations—Youth

The following guidelines for prepubescent strength training were formulated in August 1985 through joint efforts of the American Orthopaedic Society for Sports Medicine, the American Academy of Pediatrics, the American College of Sports Medicine, the Society of Pediatric Orthopaedics, the National Athletic Trainers Association, the U.S. Olympic Committee, the National Strength and Conditioning Association, and the President's Council on Physical Fitness and Sports.

Equipment

1. Strength-training equipment should be of appropriate design to accommodate the size and degree of maturity of the prepubescent.
2. It should be cost-effective.
3. It should be safe, free of defects, and inspected frequently.
4. It should be located in an uncrowded area free of obstructions with adequate lighting and ventilation.

Program Considerations

1. A preparticipation physical exam is mandatory.
2. The child must have the emotional maturity to accept coaching and instruction.
3. There must be adequate supervision by coaches who are knowledgeable about strength training and the special problems of prepubescents.

4. Strength training should be a part of an overall comprehensive program designed to increase motor skills and level of fitness.
5. Strength training should be preceded by a warm-up period and followed by a cool-down.
6. Emphasis should be on dynamic concentric contractions.
7. All exercises should be carried through a full range of motion.
8. Competition is prohibited.
9. No maximum lift should ever be attempted.

Prescribed Program

1. Training is recommended two or three times a week for twenty- to thirty-minute periods.
2. No resistance should be applied until proper form is demonstrated. Six to 15 repetitions equal one set; one to three sets per exercise should be done.
3. Weight or resistance is increased in one- to three-pound increments after the prepubescent does 15 repetitions in good form.

Training Benefits—Youth

When practiced properly, strength training may provide many physical and personal benefits to boys and girls. These include:

- Development of strong muscles (myoproteins) during the years of normal growth and maturation.
- Development of strong tendons, ligaments, and connective tissue (collagen proteins) during the years of normal growth and maturation.
- Development of strong bones (osteoproteins) during the years of normal growth and maturation.
- Reduced risk of tissue injury during the years of normal growth and maturation.
- Development of self-confidence and self-esteem during the years of self-identity and peer-acceptance.

- Development of useful exercise skills important for their own sake, and for enhancing physical performance in a variety of athletic activities.
- Opportunity for socialization, cooperation, and leadership with other youth strength-training participants.

Considering the relatively high benefits and low risks associated with well-designed and well-supervised strength exercise, it is a recommended physical activity for youth.

Research Findings—Seniors

Although many degenerative processes are associated with aging, most can be significantly delayed by means of progressive-resistance exercise. In fact, research indicates that seniors can reverse some of the debilitating effects of aging through regular strength training.

Evans and Rosenberg (1991) reported a 10 percent increase in muscle mass and a 300 percent increase in muscle strength after eight weeks of resistance training in 90-year-old men and women. A 24-week study by Parsons et al. (1992) showed significant improvements in strength, balance, and functional mobility among senior (ages 67 to 91) strength-training participants.

Westcott conducted two studies on senior strength training. In the first study (1993a), 31 seniors (average age 65 years) performed 25 minutes of strength exercise and 25 minutes of endurance exercise, three days a week. After eight weeks of training, the subjects added 3.5 pounds of lean weight and lost 5.0 pounds of fat weight, for an 8.5-pound improvement in body composition.

In the second study Westcott and Wessner (1993d), 85 seniors (average age 65 years) performed 25 minutes of strength exercise and 25 minutes of endurance exercise, two days a week. After eight weeks of training, the subjects added 2.0 pounds of lean weight and lost 4.0 pounds of fat weight, for a 6.0-pound improvement in body composition. As presented in table 11–2, the twice-a-week training program produced significant improvements in several fitness parameters among the senior men and women. Also, twice-a-week strength training appears to have both physiological and practical benefits (Gregory 1981; Braith et al. 1989; Faigenbaum et al. 1992).

Table 11-2   Changes in selected fitness parameters for senior men and women (mean age = 65 years) after eight weeks of a Tuesday-Thursday exercise program (85 subjects)

Fitness parameter	Before training	After training	Difference
Bodyweight	172.5 lbs.	170.5 lbs.	−2.0 lbs.
Percent fat	26.0%	24.0%	−2.0%*
Fat weight	45.5 lbs.	41.5 lbs.	−4.0 lbs.*
Lean weight	127.0 lbs.	129.0 lbs.	+2.0 lbs.*
Muscle strength	42.0 lbs.	62.0 lbs.	+20.0 lbs.*
Systolic BP	141 mm Hg	134 mm Hg	−7 mm Hg*
Diastolic BP	79 mm Hg	75 mm Hg	−4 mm Hg*

*Statistically significant ($p < .01$).

It is noted that no exercise-related injuries were experienced by the senior participants. Based on these research findings, it is suggested that a two- or three-day-a-week resistance training program is a safe, effective, and efficient means for increasing muscle mass and strength in senior men and women.

Training Recommendations—Seniors

Seniors are the age group most in need of regular resistance exercise to counteract the degenerative effects of aging. However, they are understandably skeptical of strength-training activity. It is therefore important to treat senior exercisers with respect, patience, and support. Because most older adults appreciate staff instruction, supervision, and assurance, the following senior strength training guidelines have been recommended (Westcott 1993e):

1. Clear objectives, concise directions, and one task at a time.
2. Careful instruction in exercise performance, including range of movement, speed of movement, correct technique, and proper breathing.

3. Attentive supervision during each strength-training session, with special emphasis on encouragement and positive reinforcement.
4. Emphasis on basic and brief strength-training protocols that address all of the major muscle groups.
5. Selection of low-risk exercises, preferably performed with support under the hips and behind the back.
6. Emphasis on integrating strength exercise with cardiovascular exercise, flexibility exercise, and recreational physical activities (walking, gardening, dancing, etc.).
7. Emphasis on sound nutritional practices, with a healthy balance of the four basic food groups.
8. All older adults should demonstrate strength-training competence and confidence before they may exercise independently in the strength-training facility.

All senior strength-training participants should have their physician's approval. However, properly-performed resistance exercise should not have adverse effects on blood pressure (see chapter 7). A recent study (Westcott 1993d) examined 85 seniors (average age 65 years), who did 25 minutes of strength exercise and 25 minutes of endurance exercise twice a week, for eight weeks. Their resting blood pressure decreased from 141/79 mm Hg to 134/75 mm Hg, a significant reduction in both systolic and diastolic blood pressure.

The keys to maintaining safe training blood pressures are continuous movement and continuous breathing throughout every exercise repetition. Static contractions and breath holding may cause undesirable blood pressure responses, and should always be avoided.

Training Benefits—Seniors

Older adults often feel that this is the time of life to retire from physical exercise and go out to pasture. Nothing could be farther from the truth. Loss of muscle and bone occurs at a rapid rate in older adults, and strength training is the best means for delaying the degenerative processes associated with aging. Consider the following reasons for older adults to perform regular strength exercise:

- Maintain or increase muscle mass (myoproteins), and contraction strength during the years of normal decline.
- Maintain or increase tendon, ligament, and connective tissue mass (collagen proteins), and tensile strength during the years of normal decline.
- Maintain or increase bone mass (osteoproteins), and tensile strength during the years of normal decline.
- Reduced risk of tissue injury during the years of normal decline.
- Development of self-confidence and self-sufficiency during the years of reduced independence.
- Development of functional strength for enhancing physical performance and carrying out daily tasks.
- Opportunity for socialization, cooperation, and leadership with other adult strength-training participants.

Considering the relatively high benefits and low risks associated with well-designed and well-supervised strength exercise, it is a recommended physical activity for seniors.

Twelve

Strength-training Considerations

The preceding chapters have presented essential information on strength training and muscle development. At this point you should have a solid understanding of strength fitness, both in principle and practical application. However, there are some related topics that should be considered in designing a safe and successful strength-training program. These include: (1) dietary requirements; (2) muscle strength and endurance; (3) joint flexibility; (4) warm-ups and cool-downs; (5) progress and assessment; (6) speed and power; (7) plyometric training, and (8) anabolic steroids.

Dietary Requirements

The most common questions asked by strength exercisers pertain to how much protein they need for better muscular development. This is a valid concern because proteins are partly responsible for the increased size and strength of trained muscle fibers.

While few people question the importance of protein in the diet, there is considerable disagreement over the amount of protein strength trainers should consume. The recommended daily protein requirement for adults is one gram for every two pounds of body weight. That is, an adult who weighs 180 pounds should consume about 90 grams of protein per day. This is approximately three ounces of protein, which most Americans easily obtain by following a normal, balanced diet. Persons who need to increase their protein intake can do so simply by eating more protein-rich foods such as low-fat dairy products and low-fat meats.

Extra protein is not generally utilized by the body and may be harmful to your kidneys. Even when you are involved in regular strength training you do not require additional protein if your daily diet is sound. This is due to the fact that your tissue (muscle) building processes occur at a relatively constant rate and are not accelerated by the presence of additional protein. Consequently, excellent muscle development may be attained without protein supplementation if you adhere to sensible nutritional guidelines.

A desirable diet provides the proteins, carbohydrates, fats, vitamins, minerals, and water necessary for good health. It is comprised of food from the following categories.

Category 1: Cereals and Grains

Many Americans eat too few cereals and grains because they mistakenly believe that these foods are high in fat. Actually, most of the foods in this category (cereal, bread, pasta) have very little fat. Instead, they serve as excellent sources of complex carbohydrates, vitamins, and minerals, and reasonably good sources of protein. It is recommended that you consume between six and eleven servings per day from this food group.

Biscuits	Pancakes
Bran cereals	Pasta
Bread	Pastries
Corn cereals	Rice
Crackers	Rice cereals
Flour	Rolls
Muffins	Wheat cereals
Oat cereals	Wheat germ

Obviously, foods made from grains may vary greatly in nutrition and calorie value. For example, cereals, breads, and pasta are preferable to cakes, cookies, and pies. Many cereals and grains have the additional advantage of providing fiber, which is essential for the efficient functioning of your digestive system.

Category 2: Fruits and Vegetables

Fruits and vegetables should make up a large percentage of your daily food intake. It is recommended that you consume three to five servings of vegetables and two to four servings of fruit from this food group each day. All sorts of fruits and vegetables are included in this category.

Apples	Cauliflower	Onions
Asparagus	Celery	Peaches
Bananas	Cherries	Pears
Beans	Citrus fruits	Peas
Beets	Corn	Peppers
Berries	Dried fruits	Plums
Broccoli	Grapes	Potatoes
Cabbage	Lettuce	Squash
Carrots	Melons	Sweet potatoes
		Tomatoes

Fruits and vegetables are excellent sources of the carbohydrates, vitamins, and minerals that are necessary for physical health and peak performance.

Category 3: Dairy Products

In addition to the protein sources presented in category 4, it is recommended that you obtain two to four servings of dairy products on a daily basis. The following dairy products are excellent sources for protein and calcium, essential nutrients for muscle contraction and bone formation.

Cheese (hard)
Cottage cheese (low-fat)
Ice milk
Milk (low-fat)
Yogurt (low-fat)

There has been considerable disagreement regarding the use of dairy products when training for muscular strength and definition. The major concern is over the high-fat content of whole-milk products. Because low-fat dairy products are readily available in nearly all grocery stores, there does not seem to be any good reason, other than allergic reactions, to avoid this highly nutritious food source. For example, one-percent milk supplies the same amount of protein and calcium as whole milk but has far less fat and fewer calories. It is interesting to note that the principal ingredient in most high-protein supplements is nonfat dried milk.

Category 4: Meat, Poultry, Fish, and Protein Foods

It is recommended that you obtain two to three servings per day of foods from this group.

Beans
Beef (lean)
Chicken
Egg whites
Fish
Lamb (lean)
Nuts (sparingly, due to high fat content)
Peanuts (sparingly, due to high fat content)
Pork (lean)
Shellfish
Soybeans or tofu (sparingly, due to high fat content)
Turkey

It is important to obtain all of the amino acids that are essential for protein synthesis. There are at least 10 that cannot be manufactured in your body and must be included in your diet. Although meat, eggs, and milk products supply all of the essential amino acids, no single vegetable, fruit, grain, or nut does so. Consequently, vegetarians must eat a variety of vegetables, fruits, grains, and nuts to ensure that none of the essential amino acids are excluded from their diet.

Sample Diet for Bodybuilders

Bodybuilders require a balanced diet and should follow the basic nutritional guidelines presented in the previous section. However, most competitive bodybuilders prefer to eat more protein and less fat than recommended. Without deviating too far from a sound diet, consider the following example for a bodybuilder's daily food intake.

Breakfast:	Whole wheat bread with jelly
	Wheat germ with raisins
	Low-fat milk
	Low-fat yogurt with fruit
	Orange juice
Lunch:	Tuna packed in water
	Tossed salad with oil and vinegar
	Low-fat milk
	Apple
	Banana
Dinner:	Broiled fish with lemon
	Whole grain rice
	Sweet potatoes
	Peas
	Whole wheat rolls
	Fresh fruit salad
	Vegetable juice
	Low-fat milk
	Walnut-stuffed dates
Snacks:	Low-fat yogurt
	Low-fat milk
	Fresh fruit
	Raisins, dates, and dried fruit

This sample menu is presented simply as a guideline for obtaining sound nutrition while emphasizing protein content and restricting fat intake. Of course, chicken, turkey, lean beef, or veal could be substituted for fish; and a wide variety of fruits, vegetables, grains, and low-fat dairy products could be interchanged without disrupting the basic bodybuilder's diet.

Muscle Strength and Endurance

As discussed in previous chapters, some people have low-endurance muscles and others have high-endurance muscles. However, there is a direct relationship between your muscle strength and

Table 12–1 Effects of 10-repetition and 20-repetition training on muscle strength and muscle endurance (20 subjects)

	Muscle strength (1-RM weightload)			Muscle endurance (Reps with 50% initial 1-RM weightload)		
	Before	After	Diff.	Before	After	Diff.
10-repetition training	52 lbs.	60 lbs.	8 lbs.	10 reps	17 reps	7 reps
20-repetition training	52 lbs.	60 lbs.	8 lbs.	11 reps	18 reps	7 reps

muscle endurance. When you improve muscle strength, you automatically improve muscle endurance.

Let's say that you can perform one bench press with 100 pounds (muscle strength) and 20 repetitions with 50 pounds (muscle endurance). After 10 weeks of low-repetition strength training you can perform one bench press with 150 pounds (muscle strength) and 30 repetitions with 50 pounds (muscle endurance). You are able to complete more repetitions with 50 pounds because it is now a smaller percentage of your maximum strength.

From a practical perspective, it is not necessary to train for both muscle strength and muscle endurance because these abilities are closely related. In a recent research study (Westcott 1991b), 20 women trained their left leg with low repetitions (10 reps in 40 seconds), and their right leg with high repetitions (20 reps in 80 seconds). After eight weeks of training, both legs made almost identical improvements in muscle strength and muscle endurance (see table 12–1). This indicates that both muscle strength and muscle endurance are developed by exercising to failure within the anaerobic energy system.

Proper strength training increases muscle strength and muscle endurance at the same time. As you become stronger, you can complete more repetitions with a given resistance.

Joint Flexibility

Flexibility refers to the range of motion in a joint, and is related to both injury prevention and force production. Tight joints increase the risk of injury and decrease the distance over which force can be applied. Consequently, a golfer who increases shoulder-joint flexibility will reduce the risk of injury and increase the driving distance, if other factors remain the same.

The key to joint flexibility is muscle stretchability, which is best accomplished through full-range movements. Strength exercise can be an effective means for improving joint flexibility when performed in an appropriate manner. For example, in the fully contracted position of the biceps curl, the opposing triceps muscles are fully stretched. Likewise, in the fully contracted position of the triceps extension, the opposing biceps muscles are fully stretched. Therefore, if you strengthen all of your major muscle groups through a full range of movement, you will also stretch them through a full range of movement.

It should be understood that a high level of muscle strength does not preclude a high level of joint flexibility. A well-designed and properly-executed strength-training program is useful for developing both muscle strength and joint flexibility.

Warm-ups and Cool-downs

It is generally agreed that a few minutes of warm-up activity may be beneficial to both injury prevention and athletic performance. A basic warm-up includes some light aerobic exercise (walking, jogging, stationary cycling) and some slow stretching movements for your major muscle groups.

Activities that require precise movements benefit from a specific warm-up in the form of progressively more forceful trials. For example, baseball pitchers, football quarterbacks, and shot putters warm up with a few easy throws, then gradually increase their intensity until they are throwing at full effort. In like manner, competitive weight lifters typically perform progressively heavier warm-up sets before attempting maximum weight loads.

On the other hand, if you train with 8 to 12 repetitions per set, it may not be necessary to perform preliminary sets with lighter weights. A weight load that you can lift for 8 to 12 repetitions is approximately 75 percent of your maximum resistance and should not cause injury or require special preparation. Also, when training in a slow and controlled manner, it takes about 50 to 70 seconds to complete 8 to 12 repetitions. Consequently, the target muscles experience a specific warm-up prior to the most difficult repetitions.

Although more attention is usually given to the warm-up, the cool-down that follows your workout is very important. The primary purpose of the cool-down is to return blood to your heart. When you stop exercising, blood accumulates in your legs, placing considerable stress on your heart and circulatory system. By continuing to exercise at a lower level, the muscle contractions assist blood flow and permit a gradual return to resting circulation.

The cool-down is essentially a warm-up in reverse, involving some light aerobic activity and stretching exercises. In a very real sense, the cool-down may mean the difference between leaving your workout feeling exhausted or feeling invigorated.

Progress and Assessment

Although the relationship between strength training and muscle development is reasonably stable over time, it is less predictable on a day-to-day or week-to-week basis. Generally speaking, strength improves at a fast rate during the first few weeks of training. However, as you continue to train, strength gains come more slowly. For example, you may increase your exercise resistance by 20 to 40 percent during your first month of training but only 2 to 4 percent during your third month of training.

Basically, the rule of diminishing returns applies to muscle development. At first, simple workouts produce large strength gains. Later, difficult workouts result in small strength gains. This state of affairs, known as a strength plateau, is seldom overcome by doubling or tripling your workout routine. Instead, you should periodically change the training variables to stimulate further strength improvement.

The key to continued progress is gradual improvement and sensitivity to strength plateaus. The strength-training logbook is a valuable tool for assessing your progress and for correcting small problems before they become major obstacles. The strength-training logbook should include the workout date, time, exercises, resistance, repetitions, sets, and notations, such as seat positions and technique adaptations. A sample of such a logbook is presented in appendix E.

The strength-training logbook provides a systematic means for comparing you to yourself, and that is the only meaningful comparison to make. One means for assessing progress is to ask the question, "How does my training today compare with my training four weeks ago?" Continued progress is dependent upon practicing those training procedures that appear most effective for producing strength gains, and eliminating those that prove least effective.

Speed and Power

Speed and power are often spoken of interchangeably, but they actually represent different physical capacities.

Speed

Speed is an important factor for successful performance in many athletic activities. Most of us would like to increase our movement speed (running speed, throwing speed, striking speed, kicking speed), but this is not an easy task.

Speed is a complex ability that is best improved by repeated practice efforts. Speed-training exercises should be performed as quickly as possible to produce the desired results. Because added resistance automatically slows your movement time, strength training may not be very effective for improving your movement speed. For example, soccer players who want to increase their kicking speed may perform fast leg extensions with 30 pounds. But because they cannot move a 30-pound weight load nearly as fast as they can kick a soccer ball, it is doubtful that this type of strength training will produce a faster kicking action. In addition, fast movements with added resistance place high stress on muscles, joints, and connective tissue.

Power

Power is the product of movement speed and movement force:

$$Power = Movement\ Speed \times Movement\ Force$$

According to this formula, you may improve your performance power by increasing your movement speed, increasing your movement force, or both. It is recommended that you perform high-quality skill training to improve your movement speed, and high-intensity strength training to improve your movement force. While your skill training should be specific to your athletic event, your strength training should follow the basic principles presented in chapter 6. Other things being equal, as you develop greater muscle strength you should experience greater performance power. (See appendix F for principles of force production.)

Over the past several years, coaches have learned that weight training can increase muscle size and strength without reducing movement speed and joint flexibility. Most athletic coaches therefore include some form of strength training in their sports programs. Participants in team sports (football, soccer, basketball, volleyball, baseball, softball, lacrosse, ice hockey, field hockey), dual sports (tennis, badminton, racquetball, handball, wrestling), and individual sports (track and field, cross-country, swimming and diving, gymnastics, bicycling, canoeing, golf, archery) can all benefit from well-designed strength-training programs.

Plyometric Training

Plyometric training is a means of eliciting more muscle force through rebound movements. There are two factors that enable muscles to produce more force following a quick stretching action. First, muscle tissue has the property of elasticity. Therefore, stretching a muscle is somewhat like stretching a rubber band.

Second, muscle tissue contains specialized sensory cells called muscle spindles. When a muscle is suddenly stretched, these mechanisms trigger an immediate and forceful muscle contraction known as the myotatic (stretch) reflex. This is an automatic neuromuscular reaction to prevent the tissue from being overstretched and injured.

Prestretching is a preliminary action to most forceful movements: for example, cocking your arm before throwing, cocking your leg before kicking, and squatting prior to a vertical jump.

Plyometric training utilizes prestretching movements in jumping and bounding drills. In fact, the landing phase of one jump provides the prestretching movement for a powerful second jump.

Some coaches carry this concept further by having athletes jump down from one box, then jump up onto another box. Others apply the plyometric principle to catching and throwing heavy medicine balls.

While plyometric training may be used to overload target muscle groups, it is important to avoid excessive landing forces that may cause damage to muscles, tendons, and connective tissue. It is definitely not advisable to use additional resistance (weight vests, ankle weights, etc.) when performing plyometric exercise, as this greatly increases landing forces and injury potential. It is recommended that individuals achieve a relatively high level of muscular strength prior to plyometric training.

Anabolic Steroids

Anabolic steroids are artificial derivatives of the male sex hormone, testosterone. Like testosterone, anabolic steroids promote tissue growth by enhancing protein synthesis. Under medical supervision, therapeutic doses of anabolic steroids are prescribed to patients with skeletal disorders, muscle atrophy, or deficient testosterone levels.

Persons taking steroids for the purpose of gaining muscle size and strength typically use 20 to 100 times the recommended therapeutic doses (Meintz 1988). It is estimated that in the United States, one-half million high school students use anabolic steroids (Buckley 1988), and that up to $250 million dollars are spent annually for black market steroid drugs (Dalton 1988).

These are alarming statistics—considering that illegal use and distribution of anabolic steroids is a federal crime in the United States. Even more disconcerting are the dozens of health problems associated with steroid use. In general, the medical risks are related to liver damage, cardiovascular disease, reproductive system disorders, and psychological abnormalities (Lamb 1989).

More specifically, steroid abuse may produce the following adverse effects in males and females (Beste 1991).

Negative Effects of Steroid Abuse

Males	Females
Liver bleeding	Liver bleeding
Liver cancer	Liver cancer
High blood pressure	High blood pressure
High blood cholesterol	High blood cholesterol
Temporary sterility	Temporary sterility
Increased breast size	Decreased breast size
Decreased testicle size	Voice deepening
Increased prostate size	Increased facial hair
Loss of hair	Loss of hair
Scarring acne	Scarring acne
Increased irritability	Increased irritability
Aggressive behavior	Aggressive behavior
Increased anxiety	Increased anxiety
Insomnia	Insomnia
Depression	Depression

In conjunction with resistance exercise, anabolic steroids may facilitate gains in muscle size and strength. However, the permanent health risks and medical consequences of steroid use far outweigh any temporary advantages. This is particularly true for youth, in whom steroid use can cause premature closing of bone growth plates (Goldman and Klatz 1992).

Most authorities agree that males and females can achieve significant improvements in muscle size and strength without using anabolic steroids. A progressive program of resistance exercise and a little patience are the essential requirements for attaining strength fitness.

Thirteen

Recommended Strength Exercises

Strength-training exercises should be selected on the dual basis of safety and effectiveness. In terms of safety, each exercise should provide a low risk of injury when performed properly. In terms of effectiveness, each exercise should offer a productive and progressive strength stimulus to the target muscle or muscle group.

Strength-training exercises that involve one joint action—such as leg extensions—produce curved movements and are referred to as rotary exercises. Strength-training exercises that involve two or more joint actions—such as leg presses—produce straight movements and are referred to as linear exercises.

The exercises illustrated in this chapter correspond with the joint movements addressed in chapters 5 and 6. Depending on the joint movement, a representative exercise performed with machines, free weights, or both is presented.

To avoid unnecessary repetition, the following training procedures should be applied to each resistance exercise.

- Perform the exercise in a slow and controlled manner.
- Perform the exercise through a full range of joint movement.
- Do not use assisting muscle groups to cheat weights that are too heavy for the target muscles.
- Do not hold your breath at any time during an exercise repetition. The preferred breathing pattern is to exhale during lifting movements and to inhale during lowering movements.
- Use seatbelts whenever they are provided.

It is also recommended to perform one exercise for each major muscle group, generally in order from larger to smaller muscles. That is, beginning with the legs, then progressing to the muscles of the trunk, torso, arms, and neck.

Barbell Heel Raise

Joint action:	Ankle extension
Prime mover muscles:	Gastrocnemius, soleus
Sample exercise:	Barbell heel raise
Exercise movement:	Rotary

Procedures:

- Stand with toes on platform and feet shoulder width apart.
- Place barbell across upper back and stabilize with wide handgrip.
- Raise heels as high as possible, and pause momentarily.
- Lower heels until calf muscles are comfortably stretched, and repeat.

Note:

- Keep back erect and head neutral throughout the exercise.

Weighted Toe Raise

Joint action:	Ankle flexion
Prime mover muscle:	Tibialis anterior
Sample exercise:	Weighted toe raise
Exercise movement:	Rotary

Procedures:	■ Sit on high seat with knee at right angle.
	■ Attach weight plate to foot with thin rope.
	■ Raise toes toward shins as far as possible, and pause momentarily.
	■ Lower toes as far as possible, and repeat.
	■ Repeat procedures with other ankle.
Note:	■ Keep lower leg vertical throughout the exercise.

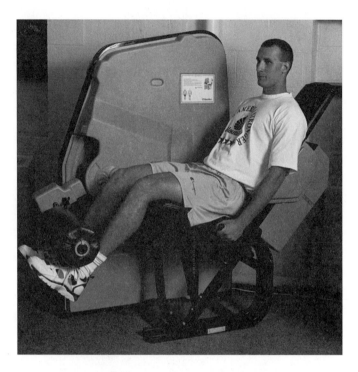

Leg Extension Machine

Joint action: Knee extension
Prime mover muscles: Quadriceps group
Sample exercise: Leg extension machine
Exercise movement: Rotary

Procedures:
- Sit on seat with knee joints aligned with machine axis of rotation.
- Place hands on handgrips.
- Place ankles behind movement pad.
- Lift movement pad until quadriceps are fully contracted, and pause momentarily.
- Lower movement pad until plates lightly touch weightstack, and repeat.

Notes:
- Keep back against seat throughout the exercise.
- Keep ankles in neutral position throughout the exercise.

Leg Curl Machine

Joint action: Knee flexion
Prime mover muscles: Hamstrings group
Sample exercise: Leg curl machine
Exercise movement: Rotary

Procedures:

- Sit on seat with knee joints aligned with machine axis of rotation.
- Place hands on handgrips.
- Place lower legs between movement pads.
- Pull movement pads downward until hamstrings are fully contracted, and pause momentarily.
- Return movement pads until plates lightly touch weightstack, and repeat.

Notes:

- Keep back against seat throughout the exercise.
- Keep ankles in flexed position (dorsi flexion) throughout the exercise.

Hip Abductor Machine

Joint action: Hip abduction
Prime mover muscles: Hip abductor group
Sample exercise: Hip abductor machine
Exercise movement: Rotary

Procedures:

- Sit on seat with hip joints aligned with machine axes of rotation.
- Place hands on handgrips.
- Place thighs inside movement pads.
- Push movement pads apart as far as possible, and pause momentarily.
- Return movement pads until plates lightly touch weightstack, and repeat.

Notes:

- Keep back against seat throughout the exercise.
- Keep ankles in neutral position throughout the exercise.

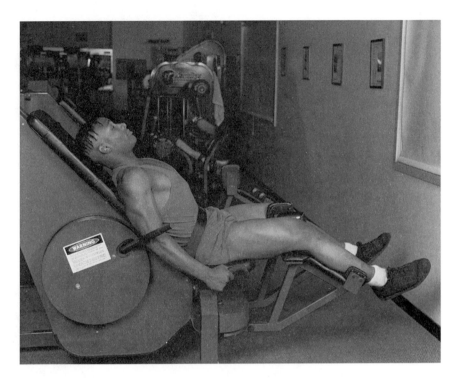

Hip Adductor Machine

Joint action: Hip adduction
Prime mover muscles: Hip adductor group
Sample exercise: Hip adductor machine
Exercise movement: Rotary

Procedures:
- Sit on seat with hip joints aligned with machine axes of rotation.
- Place hands on handgrips.
- Place thighs outside movement pads.
- Pull movement pads together, and pause momentarily.
- Return movement pads until plates lightly touch weightstack, and repeat.

Notes:
- Keep back against seat throughout the exercise.
- Keep ankles in neutral position throughout the exercise.

Leg Press Machine

Joint actions: Hip extension and knee extension
Prime mover muscles: Hamstrings group, gluteus maximus, and
                                quadriceps group
Sample exercise: Leg press machine
Exercise movement: Linear

Procedures:
- Sit on seat with feet evenly placed on movement pad.
- Place hands on handgrips.
- Push movement pad forward to near lockout position, and pause momentarily.
- Return movement pad until plates lightly touch weightstack, and repeat.

Notes:
- Keep back against seat throughout the exercise.
- Do not allow knees to reach lockout position.

Barbell Squat

Joint actions:	Hip extension and knee extension
Prime mover muscles:	Hamstrings group, gluteus maximus, and quadriceps group
Sample exercise:	Barbell squat
Exercise movement:	Linear

Procedures:

- Stand with feet shoulder-width apart.
- Place barbell across upper back and stabilize with wide handgrip.
- Lower hips until thighs are parallel to the floor, and pause momentarily.
- Raise hips upward to standing position, and repeat.

Notes:

- Keep back erect and head neutral throughout the exercise.
- Be sure to perform this exercise with a spotter.

Hanging Knee Raise

Joint action: Hip flexion
Prime mover muscles: Rectus femoris and iliopsoas
Sample exercise: Hanging knee raise
Exercise movement: Rotary

Procedures:

- Place arms on support pads with legs hanging downward.
- Raise knees as high as possible, and pause momentarily.
- Lower knees to hanging position, and repeat.

Note:

- Keep back erect and head neutral throughout the exercise.

Low Back Machine

Joint action: Trunk extension
Prime mover muscles: Erector spinae
Sample exercise: Low-back machine
Exercise movement: Rotary

Procedures:
- Sit on seat with back against movement pad.
- Place feet evenly on foot pad with knees bent about 90 degrees.
- Secure both seat belts.
- Cross arms on chest.
- Push movement pad backward as far as possible, and pause momentarily.
- Return movement pad until plates lightly touch weightstack, and repeat.

Notes:
- Keep hips against seat back throughout the exercise.
- Keep head neutral throughout the exercise.

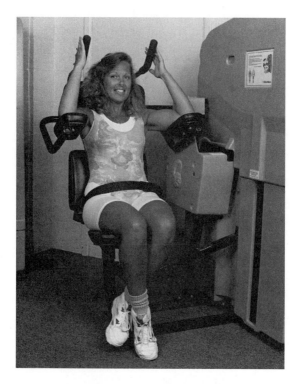

Abdominal Machine

Joint action:	Trunk flexion
Prime mover muscle:	Rectus abdominis
Sample exercises:	Abdominal machine
Exercise movement:	Rotary

Procedures:

- Sit on seat and secure seat belt.
- Place hands on handgrips and upper arms against movement pads.
- Pull movement pads downward until abdominals are fully contracted, and pause momentarily.
- Return movement pads until plates lightly touch weightstack, and repeat.

Note:

- Keep head neutral or slightly forward throughout the exercise.

Trunk Curl

Joint action:	Trunk flexion
Prime mover muscle:	Rectus abdominis
Sample exercise:	Trunk curl
Exercise movement:	Rotary

Procedures:

- Lie on floor with knees bent about 90 degrees.
- Place hands loosely on head.
- Lift shoulders off floor until abdominals are fully contracted, and pause momentarily.
- Return shoulders to floor, and repeat.

Notes:

- Keep head neutral or slightly forward throughout the exercise.
- Press low back against floor to attain fully contracted position.

Lateral Raise Machine

Joint action: Shoulder abduction
Prime mover muscles: Deltoids
Sample exercise: Lateral raise machine
Exercise movement: Rotary

Procedures:
- Sit on seat with shoulder joints aligned with machine axes of rotation.
- Secure seat belt.
- Place hands on handgrips and upper arms against movement pads.
- Lift movement pads until arms are parallel to floor, and pause momentarily.
- Lower movement pads to sides, and repeat.

Notes:
- Keep back against seat throughout the exercise.
- Keep emphasis on deltoids by not lifting arms above horizontal.

Dumbbell Lateral Raise

Joint action:	Shoulder abduction
Prime mover muscles:	Deltoids
Sample exercise:	Dumbbell lateral raise
Exercise movement:	Rotary

Procedures:

- Stand with feet shoulder-width apart.
- Hold dumbbells at waist level with elbows at right angles.
- Lift dumbbells upward/sideward until arms are parallel to floor, and pause momentarily.
- Lower dumbbells to starting position, and repeat.

Notes:

- Keep back erect throughout the exercise.
- Keep emphasis on deltoids by not lifting arms above horizontal.

Behind Neck Machine

Joint action:	Shoulder adduction
Prime mover muscles:	Latissimus dorsi, teres major, and pectoralis major
Sample exercise:	Behind neck machine
Exercise movement:	Rotary

Procedures:
- Sit on seat with shoulder joints aligned with machine axes of rotation.
- Secure seat belt.
- Place upper arms on top of movement pads in overhead position.
- Pull movement pads downward to sides, and pause momentarily.
- Return movement pads to overhead position, and repeat.

Note:
- Keep back against seat throughout the exercise.

Wide Grip Pull-down

Joint actions:	Shoulder adduction and elbow flexion
Prime mover muscles:	Latissimus dorsi, teres major, pectoralis major, and biceps brachii
Sample exercise:	Wide grip pull-down
Exercise movement:	Linear

Procedures:
- Sit on seat with feet secured.
- Grasp bar overhead with wide overhand grip.
- Pull bar downward to chin level, and pause momentarily.
- Return bar to overhead position, and repeat.

Notes:
- Keep back erect and head neutral throughout the exercise.
- Pull bar in front of face to reduce risk of rotator cuff injuries.

Pullover Machine

Joint action: Shoulder extension

Prime mover muscles: Latissimus dorsi, teres major, and
           posterior deltoid

Sample exercise: Pullover machine

Exercise movement: Rotary

Procedures:
- Sit on seat with shoulder joints aligned with machine axes of rotation.
- Secure seat belt.
- Press foot lever to bring movement pads into entry position.
- Place hands on handgrips and upper arms against movement pads.
- Pull movement pads downward until cross-bar contacts seat belt, and pause momentarily.
- Return movement pads to starting position, and repeat.

Note:
- Flex trunk during the downward movement to provide low-back support against seat.

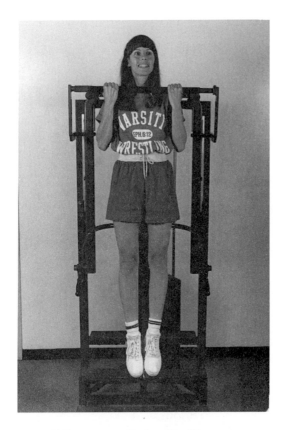

Narrow Grip Pull-up

Joint actions:	Shoulder extension and elbow flexion
Prime mover muscles:	Latissimus dorsi, teres major, posterior deltoid, and biceps brachii
Sample exercise:	Narrow grip pull-up
Exercise movement:	Linear

Procedures:
- Grasp bar with narrow underhand grip.
- Pull body upward until chin is above bar, and pause momentarily.
- Lower body to full hang position, and repeat.

Note:
- Keep body relatively straight throughout the exercise.

Dumbbell Front Raise

Joint action:	Shoulder flexion
Prime mover muscle:	Anterior deltoid
Sample exercise:	Dumbbell front raise
Exercise movement:	Rotary
Procedures:	■ Stand with feet shoulder-width apart.
	■ Hold dumbbells at sides.
	■ Lift dumbbells upward/frontward until arms are parallel to floor, and pause momentarily.
	■ Lower dumbbells to starting position, and repeat.
Notes:	■ Keep back erect throughout the exercise.
	■ Keep elbows slightly bent throughout the exercise.

Rowing Back Machine

Joint action: Shoulder horizontal extension
Prime mover muscles: Posterior deltoid, latissimus dorsi, and
                                 teres major
Sample exercise: Rowing back machine
Exercise movement: Rotary

Procedures:

- Sit on seat with shoulder joints aligned with machine axes of rotation.
- Adjust body pads for torso stability.
- Place upper arms inside movement pads and parallel to floor.
- Pull movement arms backward as far as possible, and pause momentarily.
- Return movement pads to starting position, and repeat.

Notes:

- Keep upper arms horizontal throughout the exercise.
- Keep back erect and head neutral throughout the exercise.

Dumbbell Bent Lateral Raise

Joint action: Shoulder horizontal extension
Prime mover muscles: Posterior deltoid, latissimus dorsi, and
                         teres major
Sample exercise: Dumbbell bent lateral raise
Exercise movement: Rotary

Procedures:
- Stand with feet shoulder-width apart, knees slightly bent, and back parallel to floor.
- Hold dumbbells in vertical hanging position.
- Lift dumbbells upward/sideward until upper arms are parallel to floor, and pause momentarily.
- Lower dumbbells to starting position, and repeat.

Notes:
- Keep back horizontal and head neutral throughout the exercise.
- Keep elbows slightly bent throughout the exercise.

10° Chest Machine

Joint action: Shoulder horizontal flexion
Prime mover muscles: Pectoralis major and anterior deltoid
Sample exercise: 10° chest machine
Exercise movement: Rotary

Procedures:
- Lie on bench with shoulder joints aligned with machine axes of rotation.
- Place upper arms under movement pads.
- Lift movement pads until they meet above chest, and pause momentarily.
- Return movement pads to starting position, and repeat.

Notes:
- Keep feet on floor or footrest throughout the exercise.
- Keep head, shoulders, and hips on bench throughout the exercise.

Dumbbell Bench Press

Joint actions: Shoulder horizontal flexion and elbow extension

Prime mover muscles: Pectoralis major, anterior deltoid and triceps brachii

Sample exercise: Dumbbell bench press

Exercise movement: Linear

Procedures:

- Lie on bench, and hold dumbbells at chest level.
- Press dumbbells upward to near lockout position, and pause momentarily.
- Lower dumbbells to chest, and repeat.

Notes:

- Keep feet on floor or footrest throughout the exercise.
- Keep upper arms perpendicular to body throughout the exercise.
- Keep head, shoulders, and hips on bench throughout the exercise.

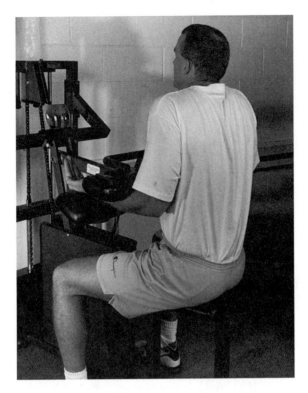

Shoulder Shrug Machine

Joint action:	Shoulder elevation
Prime mover muscle:	Upper trapezius
Sample exercise:	Shoulder shrug machine
Exercise movement:	Rotary

Procedures:	■ Sit on seat with feet on floor.
	■ Place forearms between movement pads with palms up.
	■ Lift movement pads until upper trapezius is fully contracted, and pause momentarily.
	■ Lower movement pads to starting position, and repeat.
Notes:	■ Keep back erect and head neutral throughout the exercise.
	■ Keep elbows at right angles throughout the exercise.

Barbell Shoulder Shrug

Joint action:	Shoulder elevation
Prime mover muscle:	Upper trapezius
Sample exercise:	Barbell shrug
Exercise movement:	Rotary

Procedures:

- Stand with feet shoulder-width apart.
- Grasp barbell with overhand grip.
- Lift barbell until upper trapezius is fully contracted, and pause momentarily.
- Lower barbell to starting position, and repeat.

Notes:

- Keep back erect and head neutral throughout the exercise.
- Keep arms straight throughout the exercise.

Triceps Machine

Joint action: Elbow extension
Prime mover muscle: Triceps brachii
Sample exercise: Triceps machine
Exercise movement: Rotary

Procedures:

- Sit on seat with elbow joints aligned with machine axes of rotation.
- Place side of hands on movement pads.
- Push movement pads forward until triceps are fully contracted, and pause momentarily.
- Return movement pads to starting position, and repeat.

Note:

- Keep upper arms on base pad and parallel to floor throughout the exercise.

Dumbbell Kickback

Joint action: Elbow extension
Prime mover muscle: Triceps brachii
Sample exercise: Dumbbell kickback
Exercise movement: Rotary

Procedures:
- Stand with feet staggered, knees slightly bent, and back parallel to floor.
- Place free hand on forward thigh for support.
- Hold dumbbell in hanging position with upper arm horizontal and elbow on hip.
- Lift dumbbell backward/upward until arm is parallel to floor, and pause momentarily.
- Lower dumbbell to starting position, and repeat.
- Repeat procedures with other arm.

Notes:
- Keep back horizontal and head neutral throughout the exercise.
- Keep elbow riveted to hip throughout the exercise.

Biceps Machine

Joint action: Elbow flexion
Prime mover muscle: Biceps brachii
Sample exercise: Biceps machine
Exercise movement: Rotary

Procedures:

- Sit on seat with elbow joints aligned with machine axes of rotation.
- Grasp handles with underhand grip.
- Lift handles until biceps are fully contracted, and pause momentarily.
- Lower handles to starting position, and repeat.

Notes:

- Keep upper arms on base pad and parallel to floor throughout the exercise.
- Begin and end each repetition with elbows slightly bent to reduce risk of elbow injuries.

Dumbbell Curl

Joint action:	Elbow flexion
Prime mover muscle:	Biceps brachii
Sample exercise:	Dumbbell curl
Exercise movement:	Rotary

Procedures:

- Stand with feet shoulder-width apart.
- Hold dumbbells in hanging position.
- Lift dumbbells to chest level, and pause momentarily.
- Lower dumbbells to hanging position, and repeat.

Notes:

- Keep back erect and head neutral throughout the exercise.
- Keep elbows riveted to sides throughout the exercise.

Weighted Wrist Roll

Joint actions:	Wrist extension and wrist flexion
Prime mover muscles:	Wrist extensor group and wrist flexor group
Sample exercise:	Weighted wrist roll
Exercise movement:	Rotary

Procedures:
- Stand with feet shoulder-width apart.
- Hold roller bar away from body with overhand grip.
- Turn hands clockwise until rope is fully wound on roller bar.
- Turn hands counterclockwise until rope is fully unwound off roller bar.

Notes:
- Turn hands clockwise to work the wrist flexor muscles; and turn the hands counterclockwise to work the wrist extensor muscles. (Turn hands as far as possible with each movement.)
- Keep back erect and head neutral throughout the exercise.

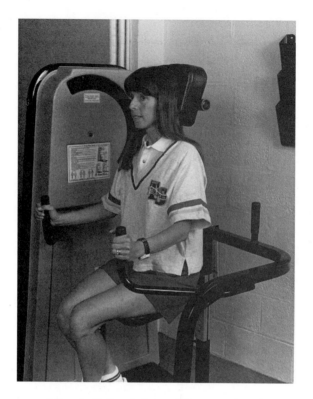

Neck Machine (Extension)

Joint action: Neck extension
Prime mover muscles: Upper trapezius and levator scapulae
Sample exercise: Neck extension machine
Exercise movement: Rotary

Procedures:

- Sit on seat with head comfortably against movement pad.
- Place hands on handgrips.
- Push movement pad backward until neck is extended, and pause momentarily.
- Return movement pad to starting position, and repeat.

Note:

- Keep back erect throughout the exercise.

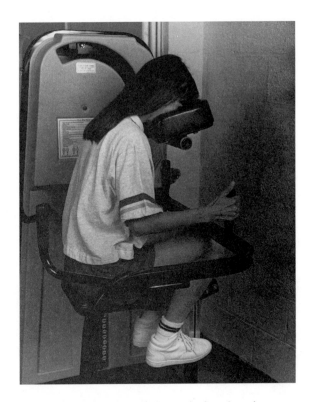

Neck Machine (Flexion)

Joint action: Neck flexion
Prime mover muscles: Sternocleidomastoids
Sample exercise: Neck flexion machine
Exercise movement: Rotary

Procedures:
- Sit on seat with face comfortably against movement pad.
- Place hands on handgrips.
- Push movement pad forward until neck is flexed, and pause momentarily.
- Return movement pad to starting position, and repeat.

Note:
- Keep back erect throughout the exercise.

Appendix A

YMCA Leg Extension Test for Muscle Strength

EQUIPMENT: Nautilus leg extension machine

PERSONNEL: One trained fitness instructor

PROCEDURES:

- Place selector pin in weightstack to lift a resistance that is about 30 percent of your bodyweight.
- Sit on the Nautilus leg extension machine with your knee joints in line with the machine axis of rotation. Place your ankles behind the roller pad, and place your hands on the handgrips.
- Perform ten slow repetitions in the following manner:

1. Lift the roller pad in two seconds to full knee extension.
2. Hold the fully contracted position for one second.
3. Lower the roller pad in four seconds until the weightstack lightly touches.

- If you complete ten repetitions, place selector pin in weightstack to lift about 40 to 50 percent of your bodyweight. After a two-minute rest, perform ten slow repetitions in the same manner as before.
- If you complete ten repetitions, place selector pin in weightstack to lift about 60 to 70 percent of your

bodyweight. After a two-minute rest, perform ten slow repetitions in the same manner as before.

- Continue to test in this manner until you cannot complete ten repetitions in proper form.
- Record the heaviest weightload that you were able to lift ten times in proper form.
- Divide this weightload by your bodyweight to determine the strength quotient.
- Place your strength quotient in the appropriate strength-fitness category.

Strength-Fitness Classifications

Strength quotient	Men	Women
Low	49% and below	39% and below
Below average	50–59%	40–49%
Average	60–69%	50–59%
Above average	70–79%	60–69%
High	80% and above	70% and above

EXAMPLE:

Name:	Jane Smith	Date:	12–06–93
Age:	18	Sex:	Female
Bodyweight:	100 lbs.		

1st weightload:	30 lbs. for 10 repetitions
2nd weightload:	50 lbs. for 10 repetitions
3rd weightload:	60 lbs. for 10 repetitions
4th weightload:	70 lbs. for 6 repetitions

Heaviest weightload performed 10 times: 60 lbs.

Divided by bodyweight: 0.60

Strength quotient: 60%

Strength fitness score: Above average

Source: Westcott, Wayne L. 1986. *Building strength at the YMCA*. Champaign, IL: Human Kinetics Publishing Company.

Appendix B

Estimating Your Muscle Length

A method for assessing your muscle length involves careful observation of some prominent muscles. Although muscle length may vary somewhat from muscle to muscle, I recommend checking at least the following two muscle groups.

1. *Calves:* Standing in front of a floor-length mirror, rise onto your toes and carefully observe the lower end of your calf muscle. If the bulge stops about midway between your knee and ankle, you have medium-length calf muscles. If the bulge disappears about one-third the distance from your knee to your ankle, you have short calf muscles. If the bulge continues two-thirds the distance from your knee to your ankle, you have long calf muscles (see figure B-1).
2. *Biceps:* With your elbow at a right angle and your wrist turned inward (supinated), see how many fingers you can comfortably place between your forearm and the end of your contracted biceps muscle. If you can insert two fingers, you have medium-length biceps muscles. If you can insert three fingers, you have short biceps muscles. If you can insert only one finger, you have long biceps muscles (see figure B-2).

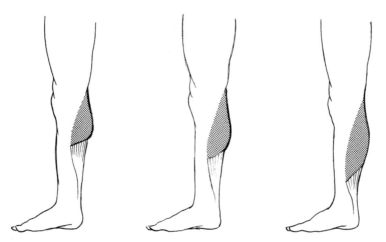

Examples of short, medium, and long calf muscles

Examples of short, **medium, and long biceps muscles**

Appendix C

Estimating Your Muscle Fiber Type

One means for estimating your muscle fiber type is determining the number of repetitions you can complete with 75 percent of your maximum resistance. Because muscle fiber type may vary somewhat from muscle to muscle, I suggest testing at least one muscle group from the lower body and one muscle group from the upper body. As an example, consider the following assessment procedure for the front thigh (quadriceps) muscles using a leg extension machine.

1. Perform 10 warm-up repetitions with a light weightload (30 percent of bodyweight).
2. Rest two minutes.
3. Perform five repetitions with a medium weightload (50 percent of bodyweight).
4. Rest two minutes.
5. Perform one repetition with a heavy weightload (70 percent of bodyweight).
6. Rest two minutes.
7. Continue in this manner until you find the maximum weightload that you can lift one time.
8. Rest five minutes.
9. Perform as many repetitions as possible with 75 percent of your maximum weightload.

If you can complete from 8 to 13 repetitions with 75 percent of your maximum resistance, you most likely have an even mix of fibers (about 50 percent fast-twitch and 50 percent slow-twitch) in this muscle group. If you complete less than 8 repetitions, you probably have a majority of fast-twitch fibers in this muscle group. If you complete more than 13 repetitions, you probably have a majority of slow-twitch fibers in this muscle group.

Appendix D

Approximate Replenishment Process for Muscle Energy Stores

(ATP–Phosphagen)

Approximate time elapsed since depletion of phosphagen stores	Approximate percentage of phosphagen stores replenished
0 seconds	0.00
30 seconds	50.00
60 seconds (1 minute)	75.00
90 seconds	87.50
120 seconds (2 minutes)	93.75
150 seconds	96.88
180 seconds (3 minutes)	98.44
210 seconds	99.22
240 seconds (4 minutes)	99.61
270 seconds	99.80
300 seconds (5 minutes)	99.90

Appendix E

Strength-training Logbook

Date _____   Start Time _____

Finish Time _____   Workout Time _____

Exercise:	_____	Exercise:	_____	Exercise:	_____
Weightload:	_____	Weightload:	_____	Weightload:	_____
Repetitions:	_____	Repetitions:	_____	Repetitions:	_____
Notes:	_____	Notes:	_____	Notes:	_____

Exercise:	_____	Exercise:	_____	Exercise:	_____
Weightload:	_____	Weightload:	_____	Weightload:	_____
Repetitions:	_____	Repetitions:	_____	Repetitions:	_____
Notes:	_____	Notes:	_____	Notes:	_____

Exercise:	_____	Exercise:	_____	Exercise:	_____
Weightload:	_____	Weightload:	_____	Weightload:	_____
Repetitions:	_____	Repetitions:	_____	Repetitions:	_____
Notes:	_____	Notes:	_____	Notes:	_____

Exercise: _____   Exercise: _____   Exercise: _____
Weightload: _____   Weightload: _____ Weightload: _____
Repetitions: _____ Repetitions: _____ Repetitions: _____
Notes: _____   Notes: _____   Notes: _____

Rest period since last workout: _____
Bodyweight: _____
Measurements: _____

Feelings: Strong   Average   Weak
               Energetic   Average   Tired
               Enthusiastic Average   Unenthusiastic

Appendix F

Principles of Force Production

There are certain basic principles of movement that should be observed when attempting to impart force to an object. The following principles of force production should be understood and applied by athletes involved in dynamic sports events.

Production of force: To apply maximum force to an object, engage the maximum number of contributing muscle groups.

Direction of force: To apply maximum force to an object, direct the force through the center of mass of the body and of the object.

Summation of force: To apply maximum force to an object, begin each successive force at the height of the previous force.

Transfer of weight: To apply maximum force to an object, move the center of mass in the direction of the force.

Range of movement: To apply maximum force to an object, accelerate the object over the maximum possible distance.

Speed of movement: To apply maximum force to an object, accelerate the object in the shortest possible time.

Action-reaction: To apply maximum force to an object, maintain contact with the ground while the object is being accelerated.

Stretch reaction: To develop maximum force, precede each muscular contraction with an initial stretch.

Absorption of force: To absorb an impact, spread the force over the maximum area and the maximum distance possible.

Glossary

Abduction: Sideward movement away from the midline of the body.

Adduction: Sideward movement toward the midline of the body.

Adenosine Triphosphate (ATP):   The chemical compound that, when split, produces energy for muscular contraction.

Aerobic: Activities that require large amounts of oxygen to produce energy for sustained periods of exercise.

Anaerobic Glycolysis: The breakdown of glycogen in the absence of oxygen to produce energy for vigorous activity lasting between 30 seconds to 3 minutes.

Antagonist muscle: Muscle that lengthens as the prime mover muscle shortens. The triceps is the antagonist muscle to the biceps.

Assisted training: An advanced strength-training technique in which a partner helps the exerciser perform a few additional lifts at the completion of the exercise set.

Atrophy: Decrease in the cross-sectional size of a muscle.

Berger program: A system of strength training in which the exerciser performs three sets of six repetitions each. All three sets are done with the 6-RM weightload.

Bodybuilder: Person who follows a strength-training program designed to develop greater muscle size.

Body composition: The ratio of lean weight (muscle, bone, etc.) to fat weight. Ideally males should be less than 15 percent fat and females should be less than 20 percent fat.

Bodyweight exercises: Exercises such as push-ups and chin-ups, in which one's bodyweight serves as the resistance.

Breakdown training: A strength-training technique characterized by immediately reducing the resistance at the point of muscle failure, and performing a few additional repetitions to further stress the muscles.

Circuit training: A training program in which one moves immediately from an exercise for one muscle group (e.g., shoulders) to an exercise for a different muscle group (e.g., abdominals), and so on until each major muscle group has been worked.

Concentric contraction: The muscle exerts force, shortens and overcomes the resistance. Also known as a positive contraction.

Controlled movement speed: A weightload is raised and lowered in a slow and controlled manner to provide consistent application of force throughout the exercise movement.

DeLorme-Watkins program: A system of strength training in which the exerciser performs three sets of ten repetitions each. The first set is done with 50 percent of the 10-RM weightload, the second set is executed with 75 percent of the 10-RM weightload, and the third set is completed with 100 percent of the 10-RM weightload.

Diastolic blood pressure: The lowest pressure inside the artery walls associated with the resting phase of the heart (diastole).

Direct resistance: The resistive force is applied to the same body segment (e.g., upper arm) to which the movement force is applied.

Dynamic-constant resistance exercise: Training with a resistance that does not change throughout the movement range, such as a barbell.

Dynamic-variable resistance exercise: Training with a resistance that changes in a predetermined manner throughout the movement range, such as a Nautilus machine.

Eccentric contraction: The muscle exerts force, lengthens, and is overcome by the resistance. Also known as a negative contraction.

Endurance: A measure of one's ability to continue exercising with a given, submaximum workload.

Extension: A movement that increases the joint angle between adjacent body parts.

Fasiculi: Groups of muscle fibers bound together by a membrane called perimysium.

Fast-twitch muscle fibers: Fibers that prefer anaerobic energy sources to produce relatively high levels of force for relatively short periods of time.

First-class lever: Lever arrangement in which the axis of rotation is between the movement force and the resistance force.

Flexion: A movement that decreases the joint angle between adjacent body parts.

Free weights: Hand-held weights, such as barbells and dumbbells, that may be moved in virtually any direction without restriction.

Full movement range: Working a muscle through a complete range of joint motion, from flexion to extension and extension to flexion.

Fusiform: Muscles characterized by relatively long fibers that run parallel to the line of pull.

High-endurance muscles: Muscles characterized by a large percentage of slow-twitch fibers that are more resistant to fatigue.

Hypertrophy: Increase in cross-sectional muscle size.

Isokinetic exercise: Training with equipment that automatically matches the resistance force to the muscle force to maintain a constant movement speed. The amount of muscle force applied determines the amount of resistance force encountered. More muscle force produces more resistance force, and less muscle force produces less resistance force.

Isometric exercise: Training in which the muscle force equals the resistance force in a static position. There is muscle tension but no muscle movement.

Isotonic exercise: Training with equipment that provides dynamic-constant resistance or dynamic-variable resistance. The amount of resistance force selected determines the amount of muscle force produced.

Lactic acid: A fatigue-producing by-product of anaerobic glycolysis.

Low-endurance muscles: Muscles characterized by a high percentage of fast-twitch fibers that are less resistant to fatigue.

Maximum heart rate: The fastest rate that one's heart will contract. Maximum heart rate can be estimated by subtracting one's age from 220.

Maximum oxygen uptake: Often referred to as Max VO_2, this represents the greatest amount of oxygen one can utilize during high levels of endurance exercise.

Momentum: The quantity of motion determined by an object's mass and velocity.

Motor unit: A single motor nerve and all of the individual muscle fibers that it activates.

Multimuscle exercise: An exercise that involves two or more major muscle groups. Linear movements such as bench presses and squats are multimuscle exercises.

Muscle adaptation: The ability of a muscle to respond positively to a slightly greater training stimulus, becoming larger and stronger.

Muscle balance: Training all of the major muscle groups so that a desirable strength relationship is maintained between opposing muscles.

Muscle contractibility: The ability of muscle tissue to shorten when stimulated to do so.

Muscle density: The relationship of muscle tissue and fat tissue within a muscle area. Low-density muscle areas contain large amounts of fat. High-density muscle areas contain small amounts of fat.

Muscle elasticity: The ability of muscle tissue to return to its normal resting length.

Muscle endurance (absolute): The number of repetitions completed with a given resistance (e.g., barbell curls with 50 pounds).

Muscle endurance (relative): The number of repetitions completed with a given percentage of maximum resistance (e.g., barbell curls with 75 percent of maximum resistance).

Muscle extensibility: The ability of muscle tissue to stretch beyond its normal resting length.

Muscle fatigue: The point in an exercise set when the muscle can no longer contract concentrically and overcome the resistance. Sometimes referred to as muscle failure.

Muscle fiber: Groups of myofibrils bound together into a functional unit and innervated by a motor nerve.

Muscle isolation: An attempt to exercise one muscle or muscle group at a time, by using rotary movements such as leg extensions and leg curls.

Muscle length: The actual length of the muscle between its tendon attachments. Relatively long muscles have greater size potential than relatively short muscles.

Muscle pump: A temporary increase in muscle cross-sectional size due to blood/fluid congestion in the muscle tissue during high-intensity training.

Muscle strength: The ability to exert muscle force against resistance force. Strength is typically measured by the maximum resistance that can be performed one time in a controlled concentric contraction.

Myofibrils: Small cylindrical protein strands that run lengthwise within each muscle fiber, and that are composed of adjacent sarcomeres.

Negative training: Advanced technique that emphasizes the negative (eccentric) phase of exercise to produce greater force output.

Olympic lifters: Athletes who strength train primarily to lift heavier weights in their competitive events—the clean and jerk, and the snatch.

Overload: Using progressively more resistance to stimulate positive strength adaptations. Overload is a relative term as a true overload would not permit concentric muscle contractions.

Overtraining: Training that does not allow the muscles to fully recover and build to slightly higher strength levels between exercise sessions. Usually rectified by reducing the training volume or taking longer recovery periods between workouts.

Paired exercises: Following an exercise for a given muscle group with an exercise for the antagonistic muscle group. For example, performing leg curls (hamstrings) upon completing leg extensions (quadriceps).

Penniform: Muscles characterized by relatively short fibers that run diagonally to the line of pull.

Phosphagen: The primary source of energy for vigorous activity of a few seconds' duration.

Postpubertal: Postpubertal refers to young men and women who have reached sexual maturity, or puberty.

Power: The rate of work production, power is the product of movement force and movement speed.

Powerlifters: Athletes who strength train primarily to lift heavier weights in their competitive events—the squat, bench press, and dead lift.

Prepubertal: Prepubertal refers to children who have not reached sexual maturity, or puberty.

Prime mover muscle: The muscle primarily responsible for performing a particular movement. The biceps are prime mover muscles for elbow flexion.

Progressive-resistance exercise: A training program in which the exercise resistance is gradually increased as the muscles become stronger.

Reciprocal inhibition: The blocking of nerve impulses to muscles that oppose a desired movement.

Recovery time: May refer to the rest period between successive exercise sets (set recovery), or the rest period between successive workouts (workout recovery).

Repetitions: The number of times an exercise is performed without interruption. Lifting the barbell from the standards, performing ten squats, then returning it to the standards constitutes one set of ten repetitions.

Rotary movement: Movement in a circular pathway, ideally with the resistance axis of rotation in line with the joint axis of rotation.

Sarcomere: The smallest functional unit of muscle contraction, a sarcomere consists of thin actin filaments, thick myosin filaments, and tiny cross-bridges that serve as coupling agents between these two protein structures.

Second-class lever: Lever arrangement in which the resistance force is between the axis of rotation and the movement force.

Set: The number of separate bouts of exercise completed. Performing ten curls, resting 60 seconds, then performing ten more curls constitutes two sets of ten repetitions each.

Slow training: A technique typically characterized by ten-second lifting movements to decrease momentum and increase muscle tension.

Slow-twitch muscle fibers: Fibers that prefer aerobic energy sources to produce relatively low levels of force for relatively long periods of time.

Spotter: A training partner who provides assistance, encouragement, feedback, and reinforcement during strength-training sessions. Spotters should always be present during high-risk exercises such as bench presses and squats for safety purposes. They also may help with high-intensity training procedures.

Stabilizer muscles: Muscles that stabilize one particular joint so that the desired movement can occur in another joint. The low-back muscles help stabilize the torso during standing barbell curls.

Strength: The ability to exert muscle force against resistance force. Strength is typically measured by the amount of resistance force that is overcome.

Strength plateau: A period of time during which no further strength gains occur. A plateau indicates that some aspect of the training program should be changed to enable further progress.

Stress adaptation: The ability of muscle tissue to make positive strength adaptations to progressively greater training demands.

Stress intensification: Gradually increasing the muscle demands by training with more resistance, more repetitions, slower movements, high-intensity techniques, or other means for making the exercise more difficult.

Super-set training: A technique characterized by performing two or more different exercises for a target muscle group. For example, a set of triceps pressdowns followed immediately by a set of dips for the triceps muscles.

Systolic blood pressure: The highest pressure inside the artery walls associated with the pumping phase of the heart (systole).

Third-class lever: Lever arrangement in which the movement force is between the axis of rotation and the resistance force.

Training duration: May apply to the elapsed time for a training set (set duration), or the elapsed time for a training session (workout duration).

Training intensity: The degree of effort necessary to complete an exercise set or an exercise session. High-intensity training is characterized by high levels of muscle fatigue.

Training principles: Research-based guidelines for developing muscle strength in a safe and effective manner.

Training specificity: Training in a particular manner to attain desired results: For example, taking short rests between sets to increase muscle hypertrophy.

Training volume: The total amount of work accomplished (weight lifted) during a training session. One means of estimating training volume is to multiply each exercise weightload by the number of repetitions completed and summing the totals.

Valsalva response: Holding the breath while working against a resistance increases chest pressure which may restrict blood return to the heart and greatly evaluate blood pressure.

Variable-resistance training: Training on an apparatus that automatically changes the resistance throughout the exercise range of movement to better match muscle force and resistance force.

Work: The product of the resistance force (weightload) times the distance it is moved. Bench pressing 200 pounds two feet represents 400 foot-pounds of work.

Bibliography

American College of Sports Medicine. 1990. The recommended quantity and quality of exercise for developing and maintaining cardiorespiratory and muscular fitness in healthy adults. *Medicine and Science in Sports and Exercise,* 22:265–274.

Atha, J. 1981. Strengthening muscle. *Exercise and Sport Science Reviews,* 9, 1–73.

Berger, Richard A. 1962a. Effects of varied weight training programs on strength. *Research Quarterly,* 33:168–181.

Berger, Richard A. 1962b. Optimum repetitions for the development of strength. *Research Quarterly,* 33:334–338.

Berger, Richard A. 1963. Comparative effects of three weight training programs. *Research Quarterly,* 34:396–397.

Beste, Alan. 1991. Steroids: You make the choice. *Iowa High School Athletic Association,* Des Moines, Iowa.

Braith, R. W., Graves, J. E., Pollock, M. L., et al. 1989. Comparison of two versus three days per week of variable resistance training during 10 and 18 week programs. *International Journal of Sports Medicine,* 10:450–454.

Buckley, William E. 1988. Estimated prevalence of anabolic steroid use among male high school seniors. *Journal of the American Medical Association,* 260:3441–3445 (December).

Clark, Nancy. 1985. Calorie adaptations to exercise. *Boston Running News,* 3: 14–15.

Counsilman, J. 1976. The importance of speed in exercise. *Scholastic Coach,* 46:94–99.

Coyle, E. F., Feiring, D. C., Rotkis, T. C., et al. 1981. Specificity of power improvements through slow and fast isokinetic training. *Journal of Applied Physiology,* 51:1437–1442.

Dalton, Bill. 1988. Steroids: From muscle to madness. *Kansas City Star Special Report,* August 28–30.

DeLorme, Thomas L., and Watkins, Arthur L. 1948. Techniques of progressive resistance exercise. *Archives of Physical Medicine,* 29:263.

Evans, William and Rosenberg, Irwin. 1991. *Biomarkers: The 10 Determinants of Aging You Can Control.* New York: Simon and Schuster.

Faigenbaum, A., Zaichkowsky, L., Westcott, W., Micheli, L., and Fehlandt, A. 1992. Effects of twice per week strength training program on children. Paper presented at Annual Meeting of New England Chapter of American College of Sports Medicine, Boxborough, MA, November 12.

Fleck, S. J., and Kraemer, W. J. 1987. *Designing Resistance Training Programs.* Champaign, IL: Human Kinetics Publishing Company.

Fleck, Steven J., Pattany, Pradip M., Stone, Michael H., Kraemer, William J., Thrush, John, and Wong, Keith. 1993. Magnetic resonance imaging determination of left ventricular mass: junior Olympic weightlifters. *Medicine and Science in Sports and Exercise,* 25:522–527.

Freedson, P., Chang, B., and Katch, F. 1984. Intra-arterial blood pressure during free-weight and hydraulic resistive exercise. *Medicine and Science in Sports and Exercise,* 16:131.

Fukunaga, T. 1976. Die absolute muskelkraft und das muskelkraft-training. *Sportarzt und Sportmed,* 11:255–265. As reported in McDonagh, M. J. N., and Davies, C. T. M. 1984. Adaptive response of mammalian skeletal muscle to exercise with high loads. *European Journal of Applied Physiology,* 52:139–155.

Gettman, L. R., and Ayres, J. 1978. Aerobic changes through 10 weeks of slow and fast isokinetic training (abstract). *Medicine and Science in Sports,* 10:47.

Goldberg, L., Schutz, R., and Kloster, F. 1983. Improvement in cardiovascular response to exercise after weight training. *Clinical Research,* 31:9.

Goldberg, L., Elliot, D., Schutz, R., and Kloster, F. 1984. Changes in lipid and lipoprotein levels after weight training. *Journal of the American Medical Association,* 252:504–506.

Goldman, Bob and Klatz, Ronald. 1992. *Death in the Locker Room II.* Chicago, IL: Elite Sports Medical Publications Inc.

Gregory, Larry W. 1981. Some observations on strength training and assessment. *The Journal of Sports Medicine and Physical Fitness,* 21:130–137 (December).

Hagberg, J. M., Eksani, A. A., Goldring, O., et al. 1984. Effect of weight training on blood pressure and hemodynamics in hypertensive adolescents. *Journal of Pediatrics,* 104:147–151.

Hakkinen, K., and Komi, P. 1983. Electromyographic changes during strength training and detraining. *Medicine and Science in Sports and Exercise,* 15:455–460.

Harris, Kathryn A., and Holly, Robert G. 1987. Physiological response to circuit weight training in borderline hypertensive subjects. *Medicine and Science in Sports and Exercise,* 19:246–252.

Hempel, Linda S., and Wells, Christine L. 1985. Cardiorespiratory cost of the Nautilus express circuit. *The Physician and Sportsmedicine,* 13:82–97.

Hunter, G. R., and McCarthy, J. P. 1982. Pressure response associated with high-intensity anaerobic training. *The Physician and Sportsmedicine,* 11:151–162.

Hurley, B. F., Hagberg, J. M., Goldberg, A. P., et al. 1988. Resistive training can reduce coronary risk factors without altering VO2 max or percent body fat. *Medicine and Science in Sports and Exercise,* 20:150–154.

Hurley, B. F., Seals, D. R., Ehsani, A. A., Cartier, L. J., et al. 1984. Effects of high-intensity strength training on cardiovascular function. *Medicine and Science in Sports and Exercise,* 16:483–488.

Ikai, M., and Fukunaga, T. 1970. A study on training effect on strength per unit cross-sectional area of muscle by means of ultrasonic measurement. *European Journal of Applied Physiology,* 28:173–180.

Johnson, B. L. 1972. Eccentric vs. concentric muscle training for strength development. *Medicine and Science in Sports*, 4:111–115.

Johnson, C. C., Stone, M. H., Lopez, A., Hebert, J. A., and Kilgore, I. T. 1982. Diet and exercise in middle-aged men. *Journal of the American Dietetic Association*, 81:695–701.

Johnson, LaVon. 1986. The role of muscle in high-level wellness. *The Winning Edge*, 5:1, 5, 12 (March–April).

Jones, Arthur. 1986. Exercise 1986: The present state of the art; now a science. *Club Industry*, 2:36A–64A.

Kelemen, Michael H., Stewart, Kerry J., Gillilan, Ronald E., et al. 1986. Circuit weight training in cardiac patients. *Journal of the American College of Cardiology*, 7:8–42 (January).

Lamb, L. 1985. Understanding calorie use and loss. *The Health Letter*, 27:1–4 (February).

Lamb, L. 1988. *The Weighting Game*. Secaucus, NJ: Carol Publishing Group.

Lamb, David R. 1989. The consequences of anabolic steroid abuse. *Gatorade Sports Science Institute Report* (February).

MacDougall, J. D., Tuxen, D., Sale, D., Sexton, A., Moroz, J., and Sutton, J. 1983. Direct measurement of arterial blood pressure during heavy resistance training. *Medicine and Science in Sports and Exercise*, 15:158.

McDonagh, M. J., and Davies, C. T. 1984. Adaptive response of mammalian skeletal muscles to exercise with high loads. *European Journal of Applied Physiology*, 52:139–155.

Meintz, Erik K. 1988. Steroids are big trouble. *American School and University*, October: 42a–42c.

Messier, Stephen P., and Dill, Mary. 1985. Alterations in strength and maximal oxygen uptake consequent to Nautilus circuit weight training. *Research Quarterly for Exercise and Sport*, 56:345–351.

Moffroid, Mary T., and Whipple, Robert H. 1970. Specificity of speed and exercise. *Journal of the American Physical Therapy Association*, 50:1692–1699.

Morganroth, J., Maron, B., Henry, W., and Epstein, S. 1975. Comparative left ventricular dimensions in trained athletes. *Annals of International Medicine*, 82: 521–524.

Moritani, T., and DeVries, H. 1979. Neural factors versus hypertrophy in the time course of muscle strength gain. *American Journal of Physical Medicine*, 58:115–130.

Munnings, Frances. 1993. Strength training: Not only for the young. *The Physician and Sportsmedicine*, 21:133–140.

National Strength and Conditioning Association. 1985. Position paper on prepubescent strength training. *National Strength and Conditioning Association Journal*, 7:27–31.

O'Shea, Patrick. 1966. Effects of selected weight training programs on the development of muscle hypertrophy. *Research Quarterly*, 37:95.

Palmieri, Gerard A. 1987. Weight training and repetition speed. *Journal of Applied Sport Science Research*, 1:36–38.

Parsons, D., Foster, V., Harman, F., et al. 1992. Balance and strength changes in elderly subjects after heavy-resistance strength training, abstracted. *Medicine and Science in Sports and Exercise*, 24:521.

Peterson, F. B. 1960. Muscle training by static, concentric and eccentric contractions. *Acta Physiology Scandinavica*, 48:406–416.

Peterson, James A. 1976. The effect of high-intensity weight training on cardiovascular function. Paper presented at International Congress of Physical Activity Sciences, Quebec City, Canada, July 15.

Pipes, T. V. 1979. High intensity, not high speed. *Athletic Journal*, 59:60–62.

Ricci, G., Lajoie, D., and Petitelerc, R. 1982. Left ventricular size following endurance, sprint, and strength training. *Medicine and Science in Sports and Exercise*, 14:344–347.

Rosentswieg, Joel, Hinson, Marilyn, and Ridgway, M. 1975. An electromyographic comparison of an isokinetic bench press performed at three speeds. *The Research Quarterly*, 46:471–475 (December).

Schantz, P. 1982. Capillary supply in hypertrophied human skeletal muscle. *Acta Physiologica Scandinavia*, 114:635–637.

Servedio, F., Bartels, R., Hamlin, R. et al. 1985. The effects of weight training using Olympic style lifts on various physiological variables in pre-pubescent boys. *Medicine and Science in Sports and Exercise*, 17:288 (April).

Sewall, Les and Micheli, Lyle J. 1986. Strength training for children. *Journal of Pediatric Orthopedics*, 6:143–146.

Stone, M. H., Blessing, D., Byrd, R., Tew, J., and Boatwright, D. 1982. Physiological effects of a short-term resistive training program on middle-aged untrained men. *National Strength and Conditioning Association Journal*, 4:16–20.

Stone, Michael H., Wilson, G. D., and Blessing, D. 1983. Cardiovascular responses to short-term Olympic style weight training in young men. *Canadian Journal of Applied Sport Science*, 8:134–139.

Van Oteghen, Sharon L. 1975. Two speeds of isokinetic exercise as related to the vertical jump performance of women. *The Research Quarterly*, 46:78–84 (March).

Ward, Ann. 1988. Time course of physiologic changes during interval and steady state cycle training. Paper presented at American College of Sports Medicine Annual Meeting, Dallas, Texas, May 1988.

Weltman, Arthur, Janney, Carol, Rians, Clark B., et al. 1986. The effects of hydraulic resistance strength training in pre-pubertal males. *Medicine and Science in Sports and Exercise*, 18:629–638.

Westcott, Wayne L. 1974. Effects of varied frequencies of weight training on the development of strength. Master's thesis. The Pennsylvania State University.

Westcott, Wayne L. 1985a. Combating disappointment when strength training progress slows. *The Journal of Physical Education and Program*, 81:D14–D15 (June).

Westcott, Wayne L. 1985b. Cardiovascular fitness and strength training. Paper presented at Nautilus National Fitness Seminar, Las Vegas, NV, August 8.

Westcott, Wayne L. 1986a. Muscle development, safety make case for slow strength training. *Journal of Physical Education and Program*, 82:E14–E16 (April).

Westcott, Wayne L. 1986b. How many reps per set? *Scholastic Coach*, 56:72–73 (December).

Westcott, Wayne L. 1986c. Integration of strength, endurance, and skill training. *Scholastic Coach*, 55:74 (May–June).

Westcott, Wayne L. 1986d. Strength training and blood pressure. *American Fitness Quarterly*, 5:38–39.

Westcott, Wayne L. 1987. Individualized strength training for girl high school runners. *Scholastic Coach*, 51:71–72 (December).

Westcott, Wayne L. 1991a. Basic high intensity training for teens and adults. *High Intensity Training Newsletter*, 3:6–8.

Westcott, Wayne L. 1991b. Effects of 10-repetition and 20-repetition resistance exercise on muscular strength and endurance. *American Fitness Quarterly*, 10:25–27 (April).

Westcott, Wayne L. 1992. Strength training research: Positive emphasis or negative emphasis. *American Fitness Quarterly*, 11:16–17.

Westcott, Wayne L. 1993a. A practical approach to senior fitness. *American Fitness Quarterly*, 12:37–38 (July).

Westcott, Wayne L. 1993b. Strength training, metabolism and weight management. Paper presented at the IDEA International Research Forum, New Orleans, LA, July 20.

Westcott, Wayne L. 1993c. Strength training for adolescents and preadolescents. Paper presented at IDEA Personal Trainer Conference, San Jose, CA, March 13.

Westcott, Wayne L. 1993d. Strength Training Research. Paper presented at IDEA Personal Trainer Conference, San Jose, CA, March 13.

Westcott, Wayne L. 1993e. Practical tips for training mature adults. *IDEA Today*, 11:30 (May).

Westcott, Wayne L. 1993f. Strength Training Research. Paper presented at the IDEA World Convention, New Orleans, LA, July 22.

Westcott, Wayne L. 1993g. Strength Training Research. Paper presented at the American College of Sports Medicine Regional Conference, New York, NY, November 20.

Westcott, Wayne L., Greenberger, K., and Milius, D. 1989. Strength training research: Sets and repetitions. *Scholastic Coach*, 58:98–100.

Westcott, Wayne L., and Howes, Bernard. 1983. Blood pressure response during weight training exercise. *National Strength and Conditioning Association Journal*, 5:67–71 (February–March).

Westcott, Wayne L., and Pappas, Marilyn. 1987. Immediate effects of circuit strength training on blood pressure. *American Fitness Quarterly*, 6:43–44 (October).

Westcott, Wayne L., and Warren, Thomas G. 1985. Short rest Nautilus training can improve cardiovascular performance. *Journal of Physical Education and Program*, 81:18–19 (July).

Wilmore, Jack H. 1993. Nutrition/weight management. *IDEA Today*, 11:53–55 (April).

Withers, R. T. 1970. Effects of varied weight training loads on the strength of university freshmen. *Research Quarterly*, 41:110–114.

Wright, James E. 1978. *Anabolic Steroids and Sports*. Natick, MA: Sports-Science Consultants.

Zohman, Lenore R. 1974. *Exercise your way to fitness and heart health*. Englewood Cliffs, NJ: CPC International.

Zuti, W. and Golding, L. 1976. Comparing diet and exercise as weight reduction tools. *The Physician and Sports Medicine*, 4:59–62.

Index